THE STUDENT COOKBOOK FOR UK UNIVERSITY NEW EDITION

100+ Simple, Cheap, And Nutritious Recipes For University Life: Master Easy And Tasty Meals On A Budget, With Step-By-Step Instruction And A 60-Day Meal Plan

ELENA N. OGLEY

TABLE OF CONTENTS

INTRODUCTION

DEAR FELLOW STUDENT CHEF,

Remember when your mum asked if you could cook more than just toast? Well, mate, you're about to prove her wrong! Welcome to your new kitchen bible – the one cookbook that'll take you from pot noodle amateur to proper chef status.

I know exactly what you're thinking: "Cooking? Proper cooking? In my tiny uni kitchen?" Trust me, I've been there. My first year at uni, I burned pasta (yes, actually burned it) and set off the fire alarm trying to make beans on toast. But look at me now – writing a cookbook! If I can learn to cook proper meals, anyone can.

This isn't just another fancy cookbook full of ingredients you've never heard of and equipment you can't afford. This is your practical guide to creating proper tasty scran that'll impress your flatmates, save you loads of money, and maybe even make your mum a bit emotional when you cook for her during the holidays.

From quick hangover cures to date night impresses, from "I'm completely skint" meals to "parents are visiting" specials – I've got you covered. So, grab your wooden spoon (or whatever you've got), and let's get cooking!

HOW TO USE THIS COOKBOOK

Right then, let's get you sorted out how this book works. I've designed it to be as faff-free as possible because let's be honest – you've got better things to do than decode complicated cooking instructions.

EVERY RECIPE IN THIS BOOK FOLLOWS THE SAME SIMPLE FORMAT:

* **Skill Level:** Marked from 🥄 (dead easy) to 🥄 🥄 🥄 (bit more challenging)
* **Budget Guide:** From £ (proper cheap) to £££ (save it for special occasions)
* **Time Needed:** Both prep and cooking time, because nobody wants a surprise 2-hour cooking session
* **Equipment Needed:** Listed right at the top, so no nasty surprises halfway through
* **Ingredients:** With proper UK measurements (none of that cup malarkey)
* **Step-by-Step:** Written exactly how I'd explain it to my mate

Look out for these special features:

* 💡 **Pro Tips:** Little tricks I've learned the hard way
* [sos] **Rescue Tips:** How to save it when things go wrong
* 💷 **Money Savers:** Ways to make it even cheaper
* 🔄 **Swap Shop:** Ingredients you can switch out
* 📦 **Leftover Legends:** What to do with the extras

QUICK START GUIDE

RIGHT, LET'S GET YOU COOKING STRAIGHT AWAY! HERE'S YOUR ESSENTIAL CHECKLIST TO GET STARTED:

FIRST THINGS FIRST

1. Kitchen Audit
   * Check what equipment you've got
   * Make a list of what you need (check Chapter 1 for essentials)
   * Don't panic if you're missing stuff – we can work around it

2. Shopping List Essentials
   * Stock up on the basics (full list in Chapter 1)
   * Start with salt, pepper, cooking oil, pasta, rice, tinned tomatoes
   * Add: onions, garlic, mixed herbs, stock cubes

3. Before You Cook
   * Read the whole recipe first (trust me on this one)
   * Check you've got all the ingredients
   * Make sure you've got enough time
   * Clean your workspace (your future self will thank you)

Remember: Everyone starts somewhere, and this book is designed to grow with you. Start with the basics, and before you know it, you'll be hosting dinner parties and impressing everyone with your culinary skills!

THE STUDENT KITCHEN 101

ESSENTIAL KITCHEN EQUIPMENT LIST

Right then, let's sort out what you need in your kitchen. I'm not going to tell you to buy some fancy spiralizer or a £200 mixer – this is the real stuff you'll use daily.

THE ABSOLUTE MUST-HAVES

1. Sharp Knife (£10-15)
  * Your most important tool
  * Get one decent chef's knife rather than a rubbish set
  * Keep it sharp (dull knives are more dangerous!)

2. Chopping Board (£5-8)
  * **At least two:** one for raw meat, one for everything else
  * Plastic ones are fine and dishwasher-safe

3. Saucepans (£15-20 for a set)
  * One small (for beans, sauces)
  * One medium (pasta, rice)
  * One large (soups, batch cooking)

4. Frying Pan (£10-12)
  * Non-stick is your best mate
  * Get one with a lid if possible

5. Basic Tools (about £20 total)
  * Wooden spoon
  * Colander
  * Can opener
  * Peeler
  * Measuring spoons
  * Grater
  * Measuring jug

Nice to Have (But Not Essential)
  * Baking tray
  * Kitchen scissors
  * Tupperware containers
  * Hand blender
  * Rice cooker
  * Kitchen scales

BUDGET-FRIENDLY SHOPPING GUIDE
WHERE TO SHOP
* Discount Supermarkets: Aldi, Lidl (your new best friends)
* Regular Supermarkets: Check the 'basics' ranges
* Local Markets: Great for cheap veg, especially near closing time
* Asian Supermarkets: Brilliant for rice, noodles, and spices in bulk

MONEY-SAVING TIPS
1. Shop Smart
  * Make a list and stick to it
  * Never shop hungry (seriously, don't)
  * Check high and low shelves (expensive stuff is at eye level)
  * Compare price per kg/unit, not package price

2. Timing is Everything
  * Shop in the evening for yellow-sticker bargains
  * Buy seasonal veg
  * Stock up on non-perishables when they're on offer

3. Bulk Buying
  * Team up with flatmates for bulk purchases
  * Split large packs of meat into portions and freeze
  * Buy rice, pasta, and tinned goods in bulk

KITCHEN SAFETY AND HYGIENE

FOOD SAFETY BASICS
* Wash your hands properly (20 seconds, with soap)
* Use different chopping boards for raw meat
* Keep raw meat at the bottom of the fridge
* Don't wash raw chicken (spreads bacteria)

KITCHEN SAFETY
* Turn pan handles away from the edge
* Keep tea towels away from the hob

FOOD STORAGE GUIDELINES

Fridge Organisation (Top to Bottom)
1. Ready-to-eat foods
2. Dairy products
3. Raw meat/fish
4. Vegetables/fruits (in drawers)

Freezer Tips
* Label everything with dates
* Portion things before freezing

* Know where your fire blanket/extinguisher is
* Don't cook when completely wasted (get a takeaway instead)

BASIC HYGIENE RULES
* Clean as you go
* Wash up properly with hot water
* Change tea towels regularly
* Keep your fridge clean

* Use within 3 months
* Don't refreeze thawed food

Cupboard Storage
* Cool, dry place
* Check for moths/weevils
* Use airtight containers
* First in, first out

UNDERSTANDING USE-BY VS BEST-BEFORE DATES

Use-By Dates
* Safety issue
* Don't eat after this date
* Common on:
  * Meat
  * Fish
  * Ready meals
  * Dairy

Best-Before Dates
* Quality issue
* Usually fine to eat after
* Use your judgment
* Common on:
  * Bread
  * Tinned goods
  * Dry pasta
  * Rice

BASIC COOKING TECHNIQUES

Essential Skills

1. Chopping
* Curl your fingers under
* Keep knife tip on board
* Rock the knife

2. Boiling
* Proper rolling boil for pasta
* Gentle simmer for rice
* Don't overcrowd the pan

3. Frying
* Heat pan before adding oil
* Don't overcrowd
* Listen for the sizzle

4. Seasoning
* Season as you go
* Taste before serving
* You can add but can't take away

MEASUREMENT CONVERSIONS

TEMPERATURE
* Gas Mark to °C
  * Gas 4 = 180°C
  * Gas 6 = 200°C
  * Gas 8 = 230°C

COMMON CONVERSIONS
* 1 cup = 250ml
* 1 tablespoon = 15ml
* 1 teaspoon = 5ml
* 1oz = 28g

COMMON COOKING TERMS EXPLAINED

Basic Terms
* Simmer: Small bubbles, not a full boil
* Sauté: Fry quickly in a little oil
* Al dente: Pasta that's cooked but still firm
* Fold: Gently mix in
* Dice: Cut into small cubes
* Reduce: Boil to make the sauce thicker

COMMON INSTRUCTIONS
* Pinch: The amount you can grab between thumb and finger
* Drizzle: Light stream of liquid
* Season to taste: Add salt/pepper until it tastes good to you
* Rest: Let meat sit after cooking
* Stir through: Mix into the dish

Remember: These are your kitchen basics. Keep this section bookmarked you'll be coming back to it a lot at first, but soon it'll all become second nature. Now, ready to start cooking? Let's get into some proper recipes!

MEAL PLANNING & PREP GUIDE

WEEKLY MEAL PLANNING BASICS

Listen up! This is where you're going to save serious money and eat proper meals all week. I learned this the hard way after blowing my entire loan on takeaways in my first year.

THE SUNDAY STRATEGY

1

. Check Your Schedule
  * When are you in lectures?
  * Which nights are you going out?
  * When do you need quick meals?
  * Any society meetups or dates?

SAMPLE WEEKLY PLAN

Monday: Big batch cook (chilli or curry)
Tuesday: Leftovers from Monday
Wednesday: Quick pasta dish
Thursday: Another batch cook (shepherd's pie)
Friday: Leftovers or social night
Saturday: Treat meal/takeaway
Sunday: Meal prep for next week

BUDGET PLANNING

 Monthly Food Budget Breakdown
* Average student budget: £120-£200/month
* Weekly breakdown: £30-£50
* Daily allowance: £4-£7

2. Make Your Weekly Plan
  * Plan 5-6 days (leave room for spontaneity)
  * Include at least 2 batch-cook meals
  * Schedule leftover nights
  * Plan around your busiest days

SMART BUDGETING TIPS

1. The 40-40-20 Rule
  * 40% on staples (pasta, rice, tinned goods)
  * 40% on fresh ingredients
  * 20% on treats and extras

2. Money-Saving Strategies
  * Use cashback apps (Too Good To Go, Student Beans)
  * Get a loyalty card at your local supermarket
  * Buy non-branded basics
  * Look for yellow-sticker items

BUDGET MEAL TEMPLATES

* £2 Meals
  * Beans on toast with extras
  * Upgraded instant noodles
  * Jacket potato with toppings

* £3-4 Meals
  * Basic pasta dishes

  * Stir-fries
  * Rice and curry

* £5+ Meals
  * Proper Sunday roast
  * Date night specials
  * Group dinners

  * Soup

BATCH COOKING GUIDE

Why Batch Cook?
* Save money
* Save time
* Always have proper food ready
* Fewer takeaway temptations

BEST DISHES FOR BATCH COOKING

1. Classic Choices
  * Chilli con carne
  * Bolognese sauce
  * Curry
  * Shepherd's pie

2. Portion and Storage
  * Cool within 2 hours
  * Divide into individual portions
  * Label with date and contents
  * Freeze flat for easy storage

BATCH COOKING SCHEDULE

Sunday Prep:
2 pm: Shopping
3 pm: Prep ingredients
4 pm: Start cooking
6 pm: Portion and store
7 pm: Kitchen cleaned

FOOD STORAGE AND LEFTOVERS
STORAGE GUIDELINES

1. Fridge (3-4 days)
  * Cooked meals in airtight containers
  * Raw meat (bottom shelf)
  * Prepared vegetables
  * Sauces and dips

2. FREEZER (2-3 MONTHS)
  * Label everything!

  * Use freezer bags for flat storage
  * Remove as much air as possible
  * Freeze in portion sizes

LEFTOVER MAGIC
* Rice: Egg fried rice
* Pasta: Frittata
* Vegetables: Soup or stir-fry
* Chicken: Sandwiches or curry
* Bread: Croutons or breadcrumbs

SHARING COSTS WITH HOUSEMATES
COMMUNAL SHOPPING SYSTEM

1. The Basics Pool
* Everyone chips in £5-10 Monthly
* Covers shared items (oil, salt, toilet roll)
* One person manages the fund
* Keep receipts in a shared folder

2. Meal Sharing
* Create a cooking rota
* Each person cooks one night
* Share shopping lists
* Split costs equally

HOUSE DINNER TIPS
* Use a payment app (Splitwise)
* Plan meals together
* Consider dietary requirements
* Make it a social event

QUICK FIXES VS PROPER MEALS
QUICK FIXES (15 MINS OR LESS)

1. Emergency Meals
* Pimped instant noodles
* Fancy beans on toast
* Quick pasta dishes
* Microwave meals plus extras

2. When to Use Quick Fixes
* Late-night study sessions
* Between lectures
* After nights out
* When you're properly knackered

PROPER MEALS (30+ MINS)

1. Worth the Extra Time
* Sunday roasts
* Homemade curries
* Lasagne
* Proper stews

2. When to Make Time
* Weekends
* Batch cooking days
* Special occasions
* When parents visit

FINDING BALANCE

* Weekday Strategy
* Monday: Batch cook
* Tuesday-Thursday: Mix of quick and proper
* Friday: Quick fix or takeaway
* Weekend: Proper cooking

Remember: The key to successful student cooking is balance. Some days you'll be a proper chef, other days beans on toast is a perfectly acceptable dinner. Don't beat yourself up about it – ensure you have options for both scenarios!

Pro Tip: Keep a few "emergency" meals in your freezer for those days when cooking isn't happening. Future you will be grateful!

CHAPTER 1: FAST FOOD FAVOURITES (BUT BETTER!)

HOMEMADE CHICKEN BURGER (BETTER THAN MCDONALD'S!)

Prep: 10 mins | Cook: 15 mins | Serves: 2

Cooking Function: Air Fry

Ingredients:

UK: 2 chicken breasts (butterflied), 100g plain flour, 1 teaspoon smoked paprika, 1 teaspoon garlic powder, 2 large eggs (beaten), 75g breadcrumbs, 30ml vegetable oil, 2 burger buns (toasted), lettuce, tomato slices, mayonnaise

Instructions:

1. Preheat the air fryer to 180°C.
2. In one bowl, mix the flour, smoked paprika, garlic powder, salt, and pepper. In a second bowl, beat the eggs. Place the breadcrumbs in a third bowl.
3. Dip each butterflied chicken breast in the flour mixture, then into the beaten eggs, and finally coat with breadcrumbs.
4. Lightly brush each chicken breast with oil and place them in the air fryer basket.
5. Air fry for 12-15 minutes, flipping halfway through, until golden brown and cooked through.
6. Assemble the burger by layering the chicken, lettuce, tomato slices, and mayonnaise inside the toasted buns.
7. Serve hot with chips on the side for a proper fast food feast!

Nutritional Info: Calories: 520 | Fat: 18g | Carbs: 45g | Protein: 35g

CRISPY OVEN-BAKED CHIPS

Prep: 5 mins | Cook: 25 mins | Serves: 2

Cooking Function: Bake

Ingredients:

UK: 3 large potatoes (peeled and cut into chips), 2 tablespoons olive oil, 1 teaspoon salt, 1/2 teaspoon black pepper, 1/2 teaspoon paprika

Instructions:

1. Preheat the oven to 200°C (fan).
2. Toss the potato chips with olive oil, salt, pepper, and paprika in a bowl until evenly coated.
3. Spread the chips on a baking tray lined with parchment paper in a single layer.
4. Bake for 20-25 minutes, flipping halfway through, until golden and crispy.
5. Serve with your favourite dipping sauce for a healthier take on chips!

Nutritional Info: Calories: 180 | Fat: 7g | Carbs: 28g | Protein: 3g

QUICK PIZZA FROM SCRATCH

Prep: 10 mins | Cook: 12 mins | Serves: 1 large pizza

Cooking Function: Bake

Ingredients:

UK: 250g plain flour, 7g instant yeast, 1/2 teaspoon salt, 150ml warm water, 2 tablespoons olive oil, 200g passata, 100g grated mozzarella, toppings of your choice (pepperoni, peppers, olives, etc.)

Instructions:

1. Preheat the oven to 220°C (fan).
2. In a bowl, combine the flour, yeast, and salt. Gradually add the warm water and olive oil, mixing until a dough forms.
3. Knead the dough on a floured surface for 5 minutes, then roll it out into a large circle.
4. Transfer the dough onto a baking tray and spread the passata evenly over the base.
5. Add mozzarella and your preferred toppings.
6. Bake for 10-12 minutes until the crust is crisp and the cheese is bubbly.
7. Slice and enjoy your quick homemade pizza!

Nutritional Info: Calories: 640 | Fat: 18g | Carbs: 90g | Protein: 25g

HOMEMADE CHICKEN NUGGETS

Prep: 10 mins | Cook: 12 mins | Serves: 2
Cooking Function: Air Fry
Ingredients:

UK: 300g chicken breast (cut into bite-sized pieces), 100g plain flour, 1/2 teaspoon garlic powder, 1/2 teaspoon smoked paprika, 1/2 teaspoon salt, 2 large eggs (beaten), 75g breadcrumbs, 30ml vegetable oil

Instructions:

1. Preheat the air fryer to 180°C.
2. Mix the flour, garlic powder, paprika, and salt in one bowl. Beat the eggs in another, and place breadcrumbs in a third.
3. Dip each chicken piece into the flour mixture, then the beaten eggs, and finally coat with breadcrumbs.
4. Lightly brush the nuggets with oil and place them in the air fryer basket.
5. Air fry for 10-12 minutes, shaking halfway through, until golden and cooked through.
6. Serve with ketchup or barbecue sauce for dipping.

Nutritional Info: Calories: 420 | Fat: 15g | Carbs: 30g | Protein: 40g

BETTER-THAN-TAKEAWAY FRIED RICE

Prep: 5 mins | Cook: 10 mins | Serves: 2
Cooking Function: Stir Fry
Ingredients:

UK: 2 tablespoons vegetable oil, 2 garlic cloves (minced), 200g cooked rice (leftover or chilled), 2 large eggs, 100g peas, 100g diced carrots, 2 tablespoons soy sauce, 1 spring onion (sliced)

Instructions:

1. Heat the oil in a large frying pan over medium heat.
2. Add the garlic and cook for 1 minute until fragrant.
3. Push the garlic to the side, crack in the eggs, and scramble until set.
4. Stir in the rice, peas, and carrots, tossing to combine.
5. Drizzle with soy sauce and stir-fry for 5-7 minutes until everything is heated through.
6. Sprinkle with spring onion and serve hot.

Nutritional Info: Calories: 350 | Fat: 12g | Carbs: 45g | Protein: 10g

PROPER FISH AND CHIPS

Prep: 10 mins | Cook: 20 mins | Serves: 2

Cooking Function: Air Fry

Ingredients:

UK: 2 cod fillets, 100g plain flour, 1/2 teaspoon baking powder, 1/2 teaspoon salt, 100ml sparkling water, 2 tablespoons olive oil, 3 large potatoes (cut into chips), malt vinegar and tartare sauce (for serving)

Instructions:

1. Preheat the air fryer to 180°C.
2. Toss the chips in 1 tablespoon of olive oil, season with salt, and air fry for 18-20 minutes, shaking halfway through.
3. In a bowl, whisk the flour, baking powder, salt, and sparkling water into a smooth batter.
4. Pat the fish fillets dry, dip them into the batter, and lightly brush with the remaining oil.
5. Place the fillets in the air fryer and cook for 10-12 minutes, flipping halfway, until golden and flaky.
6. Serve the fish and chips hot with malt vinegar and tartare sauce on the side.

Nutritional Info: Calories: 480 | Fat: 14g | Carbs: 60g | Protein: 30g

QUICK BEEF TACOS

Prep: 5 mins | Cook: 10 mins | Serves: 2

Cooking Function: Fry

Ingredients:

UK: 200g minced beef, 1/2 onion (diced), 1 teaspoon cumin, 1 teaspoon paprika, 1/2 teaspoon chilli powder, 4 small taco shells, 50g grated cheese, salsa, sour cream, lettuce (for serving)

Instructions:

1. Heat a pan over medium heat and fry the onion for 2-3 minutes until soft.
2. Add the minced beef and cook for 5-7 minutes until browned. Drain any excess fat.
3. Stir in the cumin, paprika, chilli powder, and a pinch of salt.
4. Warm the taco shells in the oven or microwave.
5. Fill the tacos with the beef mixture, cheese, salsa, and sour cream. Top with lettuce.
6. Serve immediately and enjoy!

Nutritional Info: Calories: 320 | Fat: 15g | Carbs: 30g | Protein: 20g

HOMEMADE KEBAB WRAP

Prep: 5 mins | Cook: 10 mins | Serves: 2

Cooking Function: Grill

Ingredients:

UK: 200g chicken breast (thinly sliced), 1 teaspoon ground cumin, 1 teaspoon paprika, 1/2 teaspoon garlic powder, 2 large wraps, 50g shredded lettuce, 50g diced cucumber, 2 tablespoons garlic yoghurt sauce

Instructions:

1. Preheat the grill to high.
2. Toss the chicken with cumin, paprika, garlic powder, salt, and pepper.
3. Grill the chicken for 7-8 minutes until cooked through, turning halfway.
4. Warm the wraps and layer them with lettuce, cucumber, and grilled chicken.
5. Drizzle with garlic yoghurt sauce, wrap, and enjoy your homemade kebab on the go!

Nutritional Info: Calories: 340 | Fat: 10g | Carbs: 35g | Protein: 25g

CRISPY BUFFALO WINGS

Prep: 5 mins | Cook: 15 mins | Serves: 2

Cooking Function: Air Fry

Ingredients:

UK: 8 chicken wings, 2 tablespoons plain flour, 1/2 teaspoon paprika, 1/2 teaspoon garlic powder, 2 tablespoons hot sauce, 1 tablespoon melted butter, celery sticks and blue cheese dip (for serving)

Instructions:

1. Preheat the air fryer to 180°C.
2. Toss the wings with flour, paprika, garlic powder, salt, and pepper.
3. Place the wings in the air fryer and cook for 12-15 minutes, shaking halfway.
4. Mix the hot sauce and melted butter in a bowl.
5. Toss the cooked wings in the sauce mixture until well-coated.
6. Serve with celery sticks and blue cheese dip for a classic Buffalo experience!

Nutritional Info: Calories: 300 | Fat: 20g | Carbs: 10g | Protein: 20g

LOADED NACHOS SUPREME

Prep: 5 mins | Cook: 10 mins | Serves: 2

Cooking Function: Grill

Ingredients:

UK: 100g tortilla chips, 50g grated cheddar, 50g black beans, 50g diced tomatoes, 1 jalapeño (sliced), 2 tablespoons sour cream, 2 tablespoons guacamole

Instructions:

1. Preheat the grill to high.
2. Spread the tortilla chips on a baking tray. Top with grated cheddar, black beans, tomatoes, and jalapeños.
3. Grill for 5 minutes until the cheese melts.
4. Remove from the grill and add dollops of sour cream and guacamole.
5. Serve hot and dive into this cheesy delight!

Nutritional Info: Calories: 420 | Fat: 22g | Carbs: 40g | Protein: 10g

QUICK QUESADILLAS

Prep: 5 mins | Cook: 5 mins | Serves: 2

Cooking Function: Fry

Ingredients:

UK: 2 large tortillas, 100g grated mozzarella, 50g diced bell peppers, 50g sweetcorn, 1 tablespoon olive oil

Instructions:

1. Heat a pan over medium heat and brush it with olive oil.
2. Place a tortilla in the pan and sprinkle mozzarella, bell peppers, and sweetcorn on one half.
3. Fold the tortilla in half and cook for 2-3 minutes on each side until golden and the cheese melts.
4. Slice into wedges and serve with salsa or sour cream.

Nutritional Info: Calories: 350 | Fat: 15g | Carbs: 40g | Protein: 12g

HOMEMADE NANDO'S STYLE CHICKEN

Prep: 10 mins | Cook: 20 mins | Serves: 2

Cooking Function: Air Fry

Ingredients:

UK: 2 chicken thighs, 1 teaspoon smoked paprika, 1/2 teaspoon garlic powder, 2 tablespoons peri-peri sauce, 1 tablespoon olive oil

Instructions:

1. Preheat the air fryer to 180°C.
2. Rub the chicken with paprika, garlic powder, salt, and olive oil.
3. Place the chicken in the air fryer and cook for 18-20 minutes, flipping halfway.
4. Brush with peri-peri sauce before serving.
5. Enjoy with chips or salad for a homemade Nando's fix!

Nutritional Info: Calories: 310 | Fat: 18g | Carbs: 5g | Protein: 28g

ULTIMATE GRILLED CHEESE SANDWICH

Prep: 5 mins | Cook: 5 mins | Serves: 1

Cooking Function: Fry

Ingredients:

UK: 2 slices of white bread, 50g grated cheddar, 1 tablespoon butter

Instructions:

1. Heat a pan over medium heat and melt the butter.

2. Place one slice of bread in the pan, top with cheddar, and cover with the other slice.

3. Cook for 2-3 minutes on each side until golden brown and the cheese melts.

4. Slice in half and enjoy warm!

Nutritional Info: Calories: 320 | Fat: 20g | Carbs: 25g | Protein: 10g

CHAPTER 2: BROKE BUT HUNGRY (UNDER £2 PER PORTION)

SOUPED-UP INSTANT NOODLES

Prep: 5 mins | Cook: 5 mins | Serves: 1

Cooking Function: Boil

Ingredients:

UK: 1 packet instant noodles, 100g frozen mixed vegetables, 1 egg, 1 teaspoon soy sauce, 1/2 teaspoon chilli flakes, chopped spring onions (for garnish)

Instructions:

1. Boil 500ml water in a saucepan, then add the noodles and the seasoning packet. Cook for 2-3 minutes.
2. Stir in the mixed vegetables and cook for another 2 minutes.
3. Crack the egg directly into the pot and gently swirl it to cook.
4. Add the soy sauce and chilli flakes.
5. Pour into a bowl, garnish with spring onions, and enjoy your upgraded noodles!

Nutritional Info: Calories: 380 | Fat: 12g | Carbs: 50g | Protein: 12g

TUNA PASTA BAKE

Prep: 10 mins | Cook: 25 mins | Serves: 2

Cooking Function: Bake

Ingredients:

UK: 200g pasta, 1 tin tuna (in water, drained), 300ml passata, 50g grated cheddar, 1/2 onion (diced), 1 garlic clove (minced), salt, pepper

Instructions:

1. Boil the pasta in salted water for 8 minutes, drain, and set aside.
2. In a pan, sauté the onion and garlic for 3 minutes until softened.
3. Add the passata, tuna, salt, and pepper. Simmer for 5 minutes.
4. Mix the sauce with the pasta and transfer to a baking dish.
5. Sprinkle with cheddar and bake at 180°C for 12-15 minutes until golden.
6. Serve hot, straight from the dish.

Nutritional Info: Calories: 420 | Fat: 10g | Carbs: 55g | Protein: 25g

LENTIL AND VEGETABLE CURRY

Prep: 10 mins | Cook: 30 mins | Serves: 2

Cooking Function: Simmer

Ingredients:

UK: 150g red lentils, 1 onion (diced), 1 garlic clove (minced), 1 carrot (chopped), 1 courgette (sliced), 400ml coconut milk, 2 teaspoons curry powder, salt

Instructions:

1. Rinse the lentils thoroughly and set them aside.
2. In a large pot, sauté the onion and garlic for 3-4 minutes.
3. Add the carrot, courgette, curry powder, and a pinch of salt. Stir well.
4. Pour in the coconut milk and lentils, and simmer for 20-25 minutes until thickened.
5. Serve hot with rice or naan bread.

Nutritional Info: Calories: 380 | Fat: 18g | Carbs: 40g | Protein: 15g

BUDGET BEAN CHILLI

Prep: 10 mins | Cook: 25 mins | Serves: 2

Cooking Function: Simmer

Ingredients:

UK: 1 tin kidney beans (drained), 1 tin chopped tomatoes, 1 onion (diced), 1 garlic clove (minced), 1 teaspoon cumin, 1 teaspoon smoked paprika, 1/2 teaspoon chilli powder, salt, pepper

Instructions:

1. Sauté the onion and garlic in a pan for 3-4 minutes until soft.
2. Add the beans, tomatoes, cumin, paprika, and chilli powder. Stir well.
3. Simmer for 15-20 minutes until the sauce thickens.
4. Season with salt and pepper. Serve with rice or tortilla chips.

Nutritional Info: Calories: 290 | Fat: 4g | Carbs: 45g | Protein: 12g

EGG FRIED RICE

Prep: 5 mins | Cook: 10 mins | Serves: 2

Cooking Function: Fry

Ingredients:

UK: 2 eggs, 300g cooked rice (cooled), 100g frozen peas, 1 garlic clove (minced), 2 tablespoons soy sauce, 1 spring onion (sliced)

Instructions:

1. Heat a pan over medium heat and scramble the eggs. Remove from the pan and set aside.
2. In the same pan, sauté the garlic for 1 minute.
3. Add the rice and peas, frying for 5 minutes.
4. Stir in the eggs and soy sauce. Cook for another 2 minutes.
5. Garnish with spring onions and enjoy!

Nutritional Info: Calories: 340 | Fat: 10g | Carbs: 50g | Protein: 12g

SAUSAGE AND BEAN CASSEROLE

Prep: 5 mins | Cook: 20 mins | Serves: 2

Cooking Function: Simmer

Ingredients:

UK: 4 sausages, 1 tin baked beans, 1 onion (diced), 1 garlic clove (minced), 1 teaspoon smoked paprika

Instructions:

1. Fry the sausages for 5 minutes until browned, then slice them.
2. In the same pan, sauté the onion and garlic for 3 minutes.
3. Add the beans, sausages, and paprika. Simmer for 10-12 minutes.
4. Serve with toast or mashed potatoes.

Nutritional Info: Calories: 480 | Fat: 20g | Carbs: 40g | Protein: 20g

CHICKPEA CURRY

Prep: 10 mins | Cook: 20 mins | Serves: 2

Cooking Function: Simmer

Ingredients:

UK: 1 tin chickpeas (drained), 1 tin chopped tomatoes, 1 onion (diced), 2 teaspoons curry powder, 1 garlic clove (minced), salt

Instructions:

1. Sauté the onion and garlic for 3-4 minutes.
2. Add the tomatoes, chickpeas, curry powder, and salt. Stir well.
3. Simmer for 15 minutes until thickened.
4. Serve with rice or naan bread.

Nutritional Info: Calories: 340 | Fat: 8g | Carbs: 45g | Protein: 12g

TOMATO AND LENTIL SOUP

Prep: 5 mins | Cook: 20 mins | Serves: 2

Cooking Function: Simmer

Ingredients:

UK: 200g red lentils, 400g chopped tomatoes, 1 onion (diced), 1 garlic clove (minced), 500ml vegetable stock, salt, pepper

Instructions:

1. Sauté the onion and garlic for 3 minutes.
2. Add the tomatoes, lentils, and stock. Simmer for 15 minutes.
3. Season with salt and pepper. Blend for a smoother texture if desired.
4. Serve hot with bread.

Nutritional Info: Calories: 250 | Fat: 3g | Carbs: 40g | Protein: 10g

PASTA ARRABIATA

Prep: 5 mins | Cook: 15 mins | Serves: 2

Cooking Function: Simmer

Ingredients:

UK: 200g pasta, 400g chopped tomatoes, 2 garlic cloves (minced), 1/2 teaspoon chilli flakes, salt, pepper, 1 tablespoon olive oil

Instructions:

1. Cook the pasta according to package instructions.
2. In a pan, heat the olive oil and sauté the garlic and chilli flakes for 1 minute.
3. Add the tomatoes, salt, and pepper. Simmer for 10 minutes.
4. Toss the sauce with the pasta and serve hot.

Nutritional Info: Calories: 320 | Fat: 8g | Carbs: 50g | Protein: 10g

JACKET POTATO WITH VARIOUS TOPPINGS

Prep: 5 mins | Cook: 60 mins | Serves: 1

Cooking Function: Bake

Ingredients:

UK: 1 large baking potato, 50g grated cheese, 2 tablespoons baked beans, 1 tablespoon sour cream

Instructions:

1. Prick the potato all over and bake at 200°C for 60 minutes.
2. Split open and top with cheese, beans, and sour cream.
3. Enjoy your loaded jacket potato!

Nutritional Info: Calories: 350 | Fat: 10g | Carbs: 55g | Protein: 12g

BUDGET-FRIENDLY SHAKSHUKA

Prep: 10 mins | Cook: 20 mins | Serves: 2
Cooking Function: Simmer
Ingredients:

UK: 1 tablespoon olive oil, 1 onion (diced), 1 red pepper (sliced), 2 garlic cloves (minced), 400g chopped tomatoes, 1 teaspoon smoked paprika, 1 teaspoon cumin, salt, pepper, 4 eggs, fresh parsley (for garnish)

Instructions:

1. Heat the olive oil in a frying pan and sauté the onion, garlic, and pepper for 5 minutes until softened.
2. Add the chopped tomatoes, paprika, cumin, salt, and pepper. Simmer for 10 minutes until the sauce thickens.
3. Make four small wells in the sauce and crack an egg into each.
4. Cover the pan and cook for 5 minutes until the eggs are just set.
5. Garnish with fresh parsley and serve with toasted bread.

Nutritional Info: Calories: 280 | Fat: 12g | Carbs: 25g | Protein: 15g

BEANS AND RICE BOWL

Prep: 5 mins | Cook: 15 mins | Serves: 2

Cooking Function: Simmer

Ingredients:

UK: 250g cooked rice, 1 tin black beans (drained), 1 garlic clove (minced), 1 teaspoon cumin, 1/2 teaspoon chilli flakes, 1 tablespoon olive oil, 1 lime (juiced), salt, chopped coriander (for garnish)

Instructions:

1. Heat olive oil in a pan and sauté the garlic for 1 minute.
2. Add the black beans, cumin, chilli flakes, and a pinch of salt. Cook for 5 minutes.
3. Stir in the cooked rice and heat through for 5 minutes.
4. Squeeze over the lime juice and top with fresh coriander.
5. Enjoy this simple yet satisfying bowl!

Nutritional Info: Calories: 320 | Fat: 8g | Carbs: 50g | Protein: 10g

LOADED INSTANT NOODLES

Prep: 5 mins | Cook: 10 mins | Serves: 1

Cooking Function: Boil

Ingredients:

UK: 1 packet instant noodles, 1 egg, 50g cooked chicken (shredded), 1/2 carrot (grated), 1 tablespoon soy sauce, 1 spring onion (sliced), chilli sauce (optional)

Instructions:

1. Cook the noodles according to the packet instructions.
2. In the last 2 minutes, add the egg and stir to scramble.
3. Stir in the chicken, carrot, and soy sauce.
4. Transfer to a bowl and top with sliced spring onion.
5. Drizzle with chilli sauce if you like it spicy.

Nutritional Info: Calories: 380 | Fat: 10g | Carbs: 55g | Protein: 15g

CHAPTER 3: ONE-POT WONDERS

STUDENT SPAG BOL

Prep: 10 mins | Cook: 30 mins | Serves: 4

Cooking Function: Boil and Simmer

Ingredients:

UK: 400g minced beef, 1 onion (chopped), 2 garlic cloves (minced), 400g chopped tomatoes, 2 tablespoons tomato purée, 150ml beef stock, 300g spaghetti, 1 teaspoon dried oregano, 1 tablespoon olive oil, salt, pepper, grated cheese (for serving)

Instructions:

1. Heat the olive oil in a large saucepan over medium heat.
2. Add the chopped onion and minced garlic, cooking until softened (about 5 minutes).
3. Stir in the minced beef and cook until browned.
4. Add the chopped tomatoes, tomato purée, beef stock, dried oregano, salt, and pepper.
5. Bring to a boil, then reduce the heat and simmer for 20 minutes, stirring occasionally.
6. Meanwhile, cook the spaghetti in a separate pot according to package instructions until al dente.
7. Drain the spaghetti and add it to the sauce, tossing to combine.
8. Serve with grated cheese on top for a delicious student-friendly meal!

Nutritional Info: Calories: 450 | Fat: 20g | Carbs: 50g | Protein: 25g

CHICKEN AND RICE ONE-POT

Prep: 10 mins | Cook: 40 mins | Serves: 4

Cooking Function: Sauté and Simmer

Ingredients:

UK: 500g chicken thighs (boneless, chopped), 300g long-grain rice, 1 onion (chopped), 2 garlic cloves (minced), 1 bell pepper (chopped), 1 teaspoon smoked paprika, 750ml chicken stock, 1 tablespoon olive oil, salt, pepper, frozen peas (for garnish)

Instructions:

1. Heat the olive oil in a large pot over medium heat.

2. Add the chopped onion and garlic, cooking until softened (about 5 minutes).

3. Add the chopped chicken thighs, seasoning with salt, pepper, and smoked paprika. Cook until browned.

4. Stir in the bell pepper and rice, mixing well for a minute.

5. Pour in the chicken stock, bringing the mixture to a boil.

6. Reduce the heat to low, cover, and simmer for 25 minutes until the rice is cooked.

7. Add the frozen peas for the last 5 minutes of cooking.

8. Fluff with a fork and serve warm.

Nutritional Info: Calories: 480 | Fat: 15g | Carbs: 50g | Protein: 35g

EASY CHILLI CON CARNE

Prep: 10 mins | Cook: 30 mins | Serves: 4

Cooking Function: Sauté and Simmer

Ingredients:

UK: 400g minced beef, 1 onion (chopped), 2 garlic cloves (minced), 1 bell pepper (chopped), 400g kidney beans (drained), 400g chopped tomatoes, 2 tablespoons tomato purée, 1 teaspoon cumin, 1 teaspoon paprika, 1 tablespoon olive oil, salt, pepper

Instructions:

1. In a large saucepan, heat the olive oil over medium heat.

2. Add the chopped onion and garlic, cooking until soft (about 5 minutes).

3. Stir in the minced beef, browning it all over.

4. Add the chopped bell pepper, cumin, and paprika, mixing well.

5. Pour in the chopped tomatoes and tomato purée, then stir in the kidney beans.

6. Bring to a boil, then reduce the heat and simmer for 20 minutes, stirring occasionally.

7. Serve hot with bread or rice!

Nutritional Info: Calories: 450 | Fat: 18g | Carbs: 40g | Protein: 30g

VEGETABLE AND BEAN STEW

Prep: 10 mins | Cook: 30 mins | Serves: 4

Cooking Function: Sauté and Simmer

Ingredients:

UK: 1 onion (chopped), 2 garlic cloves (minced), 2 carrots (chopped), 1 courgette (chopped), 400g chopped tomatoes, 400g mixed beans (drained), 1 teaspoon dried thyme, 750ml vegetable stock, 1 tablespoon olive oil, salt, pepper

Instructions:

1. Heat the olive oil in a large pot over medium heat.
2. Add the chopped onion and garlic, cooking until soft (about 5 minutes).
3. Stir in the carrots and courgette, cooking for another 5 minutes.
4. Pour in the chopped tomatoes and vegetable stock.
5. Add the mixed beans, thyme, salt, and pepper, bringing to a boil.
6. Reduce the heat and simmer for 20 minutes, stirring occasionally.
7. Serve hot with crusty bread.

Nutritional Info: Calories: 300 | Fat: 8g | Carbs: 45g | Protein: 15g

CHICKEN CURRY IN A HURRY

Prep: 10 mins | Cook: 20 mins | Serves: 4

Cooking Function: Sauté and Simmer

Ingredients:

UK: 500g chicken breast (chopped), 1 onion (chopped), 2 garlic cloves (minced), 1 tablespoon curry powder, 400g chopped tomatoes, 150ml coconut milk, 1 tablespoon olive oil, salt, pepper

Instructions:

1. In a large pot, heat the olive oil over medium heat.
2. Add the chopped onion and garlic, cooking until soft (about 5 minutes).
3. Stir in the chopped chicken and curry powder, cooking until the chicken is browned.
4. Pour in the chopped tomatoes and coconut milk, mixing well.
5. Bring to a boil, then reduce the heat and simmer for 15 minutes until the chicken is cooked through.
6. Serve with rice or naan!

Nutritional Info: Calories: 400 | Fat: 15g | Carbs: 30g | Protein: 35g

ONE-POT MAC AND CHEESE

Prep: 5 mins | Cook: 20 mins | Serves: 4

Cooking Function: Boil and Simmer

Ingredients:

UK: 300g macaroni pasta, 750ml milk, 200g cheddar cheese (grated), 50g butter, 1 tablespoon flour, salt, pepper

Instructions:

1. In a large pot, combine the macaroni and milk, bringing to a boil.
2. Reduce the heat and simmer for 10 minutes until the pasta is tender.
3. In a separate saucepan, melt the butter and stir in the flour to create a roux.
4. Gradually add the cooked pasta and milk mixture to the roux, stirring constantly.
5. Stir in the grated cheese until melted and creamy.
6. Season with salt and pepper, and serve warm.

Nutritional Info: Calories: 550 | Fat: 25g | Carbs: 60g | Protein: 20g

SAUSAGE AND BEAN CASSEROLE

Prep: 10 mins | Cook: 30 mins | Serves: 4

Cooking Function: Sauté and Bake

Ingredients:

UK: 400g sausages (your choice), 1 onion (chopped), 2 garlic cloves (minced), 400g baked beans, 400g chopped tomatoes, 1 teaspoon mixed herbs, 1 tablespoon olive oil, salt, pepper

Instructions:

1. Preheat the oven to 180°C (fan).
2. In a large oven-proof pot, heat the olive oil over medium heat.
3. Add the chopped onion and garlic, cooking until soft (about 5 minutes).
4. Add the sausages, browning them on all sides.
5. Stir in the baked beans, chopped tomatoes, mixed herbs, salt, and pepper.
6. Cover and transfer to the oven, baking for 20 minutes.
7. Serve hot with bread or rice!

Nutritional Info: Calories: 500 | Fat: 25g | Carbs: 40g | Protein: 30g

MEDITERRANEAN CHICKEN

Prep: 10 mins | **Cook:** 30 mins | **Serves:** 4

Cooking Function: Sauté and Simmer

Ingredients:

UK: 500g chicken breast (chopped), 1 onion (chopped), 1 bell pepper (chopped), 200g cherry tomatoes, 1 teaspoon dried oregano, 150ml chicken stock, 1 tablespoon olive oil, salt, pepper

Instructions:

1. In a large pot, heat the olive oil over medium heat.
2. Add the chopped onion and bell pepper, cooking until softened (about 5 minutes).
3. Stir in the chopped chicken, browning it all over.
4. Add the cherry tomatoes, dried oregano, chicken stock, salt, and pepper.
5. Bring to a boil, then reduce the heat and simmer for 20 minutes until the chicken is cooked through.
6. Serve warm with rice or crusty bread!

Nutritional Info: Calories: 400 | Fat: 10g | Carbs: 20g | Protein: 40g

VEGGIE PASTA POT

Prep: 5 mins | **Cook:** 15 mins | **Serves:** 4

Cooking Function: Boil and Simmer

Ingredients:

UK: 300g pasta (your choice), 1 courgette (sliced), 1 bell pepper (chopped), 150g spinach, 400g chopped tomatoes, 1 tablespoon olive oil, salt, pepper

Instructions:

1. In a large pot, cook the pasta according to package instructions, then drain.
2. In the same pot, heat the olive oil over medium heat.
3. Add the sliced courgette and chopped bell pepper, cooking until softened (about 5 minutes).
4. Stir in the chopped tomatoes and spinach, cooking until the spinach is wilted.
5. Add the drained pasta, mixing well.
6. Season with salt and pepper, and serve warm!

Nutritional Info: Calories: 350 | Fat: 8g | Carbs: 60g | Protein: 12g

RICE AND PEA RISOTTO

Prep: 5 mins | Cook: 25 mins | Serves: 4

Cooking Function: Sauté and Simmer

Ingredients:

UK: 300g Arborio rice, 1 onion (chopped), 2 garlic cloves (minced), 750ml vegetable stock, 150g frozen peas, 50g Parmesan cheese (grated), 1 tablespoon olive oil, salt, pepper

Instructions:

1. Heat the olive oil in a large pot over medium heat.
2. Add the chopped onion and garlic, cooking until soft (about 5 minutes).
3. Stir in the Arborio rice, cooking for 2 minutes until slightly translucent.
4. Gradually add the vegetable stock, stirring constantly until absorbed.
5. After about 15 minutes, stir in the frozen peas.
6. Once the rice is creamy and cooked, remove from heat and stir in the grated Parmesan.
7. Season with salt and pepper, then serve warm.

Nutritional Info: Calories: 400 | Fat: 10g | Carbs: 65g | Protein: 12g

COCONUT DAHL

Prep: 5 mins | Cook: 25 mins | Serves: 4

Cooking Function: Sauté and Simmer

Ingredients:

UK: 200g red lentils, 400ml coconut milk, 1 onion (chopped), 2 garlic cloves (minced), 1 teaspoon curry powder, 750ml vegetable stock, 1 tablespoon olive oil, salt, pepper

Instructions:

1. Heat the olive oil in a large pot over medium heat.
2. Add the chopped onion and garlic, cooking until soft (about 5 minutes).
3. Stir in the curry powder and red lentils, mixing for 1 minute.
4. Pour in the coconut milk and vegetable stock, bringing to a boil.
5. Reduce heat and simmer for 20 minutes until the lentils are soft.
6. Season with salt and pepper, then serve warm with rice or bread.

Nutritional Info: Calories: 350 | Fat: 18g | Carbs: 40g | Protein: 12g

SPANISH RICE

Prep: 5 mins | Cook: 20 mins | Serves: 4

Cooking Function: Sauté and Simmer

Ingredients:

UK: 300g long-grain rice, 1 onion (chopped), 1 bell pepper (chopped), 400g chopped tomatoes, 750ml vegetable stock, 1 teaspoon smoked paprika, 1 tablespoon olive oil, salt, pepper

Instructions:

1. Heat the olive oil in a large pot over medium heat.
2. Add the chopped onion and bell pepper, cooking until softened (about 5 minutes).
3. Stir in the rice and smoked paprika, cooking for 1 minute.
4. Pour in the chopped tomatoes and vegetable stock, bringing to a boil.
5. Reduce the heat and simmer for 15 minutes until the rice is cooked.
6. Fluff with a fork and serve warm.

Nutritional Info: Calories: 400 | Fat: 10g | Carbs: 60g | Protein: 10g

ONE-POT JAMBALAYA

Prep: 10 mins | Cook: 30 mins | Serves: 4

Cooking Function: Sauté and Simmer

Ingredients:

UK: 200g chicken breast (chopped), 100g chorizo (sliced), 300g long-grain rice, 1 onion (chopped), 1 bell pepper (chopped), 400g chopped tomatoes, 750ml chicken stock, 1 tablespoon Cajun seasoning, 1 tablespoon olive oil, salt, pepper

Instructions:

1. Heat the olive oil in a large pot over medium heat.
2. Add the chopped onion and bell pepper, cooking until softened (about 5 minutes).
3. Stir in the chicken and chorizo, cooking until browned.
4. Add the rice and Cajun seasoning, stirring for 1 minute.
5. Pour in the chopped tomatoes and chicken stock, bringing to a boil.
6. Reduce the heat and simmer for 20 minutes until the rice is cooked.
7. Serve warm with extra seasoning if desired.

Nutritional Info: Calories: 500 | Fat: 25g | Carbs: 40g | Protein: 30g

CHAPTER 4: TASTE OF HOME

CLASSIC SHEPHERD'S PIE

Prep: 15 mins | Cook: 1 hour | Serves: 4

Cooking Function: Bake

Ingredients:

UK: 500g minced lamb, 1 onion (diced), 2 carrots (chopped), 2 garlic cloves (minced), 1 tablespoon tomato purée, 300ml beef stock, 1 teaspoon Worcestershire sauce, 700g potatoes (peeled and chopped), 50g butter, 100ml milk, salt, pepper, 50g grated cheddar

Instructions:

1. Preheat the oven to 180°C (fan).
2. Boil the potatoes for 15 minutes until soft, then mash with butter, milk, salt, and pepper.
3. In a large pan, brown the minced lamb. Add the onion, garlic, and carrots, cooking for 5 minutes.
4. Stir in the tomato purée and Worcestershire sauce, then add the stock and simmer for 15 minutes until thickened.
5. Pour the lamb mixture into a baking dish, spread the mashed potatoes on top, and sprinkle with cheddar.
6. Bake for 20 minutes until the top is golden brown.

Nutritional Info: Calories: 490 | Fat: 24g | Carbs: 43g | Protein: 26g

PROPER SUNDAY ROAST

Prep: 20 mins | Cook: 2 hours | Serves: 4

Cooking Function: Roast

Ingredients:

UK: 1.5kg chicken (whole), 2 tablespoons olive oil, 1 tablespoon salt, 1 teaspoon pepper, 500g potatoes (peeled and chopped), 300g carrots (peeled and chopped), 200g Brussels sprouts, gravy (to serve)

Instructions:

1. Preheat the oven to 200°C (fan).
2. Rub the chicken with olive oil, salt, and pepper, then place it in a roasting tray.
3. Arrange the chopped potatoes, carrots, and Brussels sprouts around the chicken.
4. Roast for 1.5 hours, basting occasionally, until the chicken is golden and cooked through.
5. Rest the chicken for 10 minutes before carving.
6. Serve with gravy for a classic Sunday meal.

Nutritional Info: Calories: 650 | Fat: 30g | Carbs: 45g | Protein: 55g

BANGERS AND MASH

Prep: 10 mins | Cook: 30 mins | Serves: 4

Cooking Function: Boil & Fry

Ingredients:

UK: 8 pork sausages, 700g potatoes (peeled and chopped), 100ml milk, 50g butter, 200ml onion gravy, salt, pepper

Instructions:

1. Boil the potatoes for 20 minutes until tender.
2. Meanwhile, fry the sausages in a pan until browned and cooked through.
3. Drain the potatoes, and mash them with milk, butter, salt, and pepper.
4. Serve the sausages on top of the mash, drizzled with hot onion gravy.

Nutritional Info: Calories: 550 | Fat: 32g | Carbs: 45g | Protein: 20g

COTTAGE PIE

Prep: 15 mins | Cook: 1 hour | Serves: 4

Cooking Function: Bake

Ingredients:

UK: 500g minced beef, 1 onion (diced), 2 carrots (chopped), 2 garlic cloves (minced), 1 tablespoon tomato purée, 300ml beef stock, 1 teaspoon Worcestershire sauce, 700g potatoes (peeled and chopped), 50g butter, 100ml milk, salt, pepper, 50g grated cheddar

Instructions:

1. Preheat the oven to 180°C (fan).
2. Boil the potatoes for 15 minutes until soft, then mash with butter, milk, salt, and pepper.
3. In a large pan, brown the minced beef. Add the onions, garlic, and carrots, cooking for 5 minutes.
4. Stir in the tomato purée and Worcestershire sauce, then add the stock and simmer for 15 minutes until thickened.
5. Pour the beef mixture into a baking dish, spread the mashed potatoes on top, and sprinkle with cheddar.
6. Bake for 20 minutes until the top is golden.

Nutritional Info: Calories: 490 | Fat: 24g | Carbs: 43g | Protein: 26g

CLASSIC FISH PIE

Prep: 20 mins | Cook: 45 mins | Serves: 4

Cooking Function: Bake

Ingredients:

UK: 500g fish mix (salmon, cod, smoked haddock), 400ml milk, 1 onion (diced), 50g butter, 50g plain flour, 100g peas, 700g potatoes (peeled and quartered), 100ml cream, salt, pepper, 50g grated cheddar

Instructions:

1. Preheat the oven to 180°C (fan).
2. Boil the potatoes for 15 minutes until soft, then mash with some of the butter, salt, and pepper.
3. In a pan, melt the rest of the butter and stir in the flour to make a paste. Gradually whisk in the milk, cooking for 5 minutes until thickened.
4. Add the fish and peas to the sauce, cooking for 5 more minutes.
5. Pour the fish mixture into a baking dish, spread the mashed potatoes on top, and sprinkle with cheddar.
6. Bake for 30 minutes until golden brown.

Nutritional Info: Calories: 600 | Fat: 30g | Carbs: 50g | Protein: 34g

TOAD IN THE HOLE

Prep: 10 mins | Cook: 40 mins | Serves: 4

Cooking Function: Bake

Ingredients:

UK: 8 sausages, 100g plain flour, 2 eggs, 250ml milk, 1 tablespoon vegetable oil, salt, pepper, 200ml onion gravy

Instructions:

1. Preheat the oven to 200°C (fan).
2. Whisk together the flour, eggs, milk, salt, and pepper to make the batter.
3. Heat oil in a roasting tin in the oven for 5 minutes.
4. Place the sausages in the hot tin, then pour the batter over them.
5. Bake for 30 minutes until puffed and golden.
6. Serve with onion gravy.

Nutritional Info: Calories: 550 | Fat: 32g | Carbs: 42g | Protein: 23g

CHICKEN AND LEEK PIE

Prep: 15 mins | Cook: 45 mins | Serves: 4
Cooking Function: Bake
Ingredients:

UK: 300g chicken breast (cubed), 1 leek (sliced), 2 garlic cloves (minced), 100ml cream, 250ml chicken stock, 1 tablespoon plain flour, 1 sheet puff pastry, salt, pepper, 1 egg (for glazing)

Instructions:

1. Preheat the oven to 200°C (fan).
2. In a pan, cook the chicken until browned, then add the leek and garlic. Cook for another 5 minutes.
3. Stir in the flour, then add the cream and stock, cooking until thickened. Season with salt and pepper.
4. Pour the mixture into a pie dish and cover with puff pastry.
5. Glaze with beaten egg and bake for 25-30 minutes until golden.

Nutritional Info: Calories: 560 | Fat: 36g | Carbs: 30g | Protein: 35g

FULL ENGLISH BREAKFAST

Prep: 10 mins | Cook: 20 mins | Serves: 2
Cooking Function: Grill & Fry
Ingredients:

UK: 4 pork sausages, 4 rashers bacon, 2 eggs, 200g baked beans, 2 tomatoes (halved), 2 slices black pudding (optional), 4 slices toast

Instructions:

1. Preheat your grill.
2. Grill the sausages and bacon until cooked through.
3. In a pan, fry the eggs to your liking.
4. Heat the baked beans in a saucepan.
5. Serve the sausages, bacon, eggs, tomatoes, and black pudding with toast on the side.

Nutritional Info: Calories: 800 | Fat: 52g | Carbs: 40g | Protein: 45g

BEEF STEW AND DUMPLINGS

Prep: 15 mins | Cook: 2 hours | Serves: 4

Cooking Function: Simmer

Ingredients:

UK: 500g stewing beef (cubed), 1 onion (diced), 2 carrots (chopped), 2 potatoes (peeled and chopped), 1 parsnip (chopped), 1 tablespoon tomato purée, 1-litre beef stock, 100g self-raising flour, 50g suet, salt, pepper

Instructions:

1. In a large pot, brown the beef. Add the onion, carrots, and parsnip, cooking for 5 minutes.
2. Stir in the tomato purée and add the stock. Simmer for 1.5 hours until tender.
3. Mix the flour with suet, adding water to form a dough. Roll into balls.
4. Add dumplings to the stew and cook for another 15 minutes.

Nutritional Info: Calories: 600 | Fat: 30g | Carbs: 45g | Protein: 40g

LANCASHIRE HOTPOT

Prep: 15 mins | Cook: 1 hour 30 mins | Serves: 4

Cooking Function: Bake

Ingredients:

UK: 500g lamb (cubed), 1 onion (sliced), 3 carrots (sliced), 600g potatoes (sliced), 500ml lamb stock, salt, pepper, 1 tablespoon Worcestershire sauce

Instructions:

1. Preheat the oven to 160°C (fan).
2. Layer the lamb, onion, and carrots in a baking dish. Season with salt and pepper.
3. Pour over the stock and Worcestershire sauce, then layer the sliced potatoes on top.
4. Cover with foil and bake for 1.5 hours.
5. Remove the foil and bake for an additional 15 minutes until golden.

Nutritional Info: Calories: 520 | Fat: 28g | Carbs: 45g | Protein: 30g

BUBBLE AND SQUEAK

Prep: 10 mins | Cook: 15 mins | Serves: 4

Cooking Function: Fry

Ingredients:

UK: 300g leftover vegetables (cooked), 2 boiled potatoes (mashed), 1 egg (beaten), salt, pepper, oil for frying

Instructions:

1. In a bowl, mix the vegetables, potatoes, and egg. Season with salt and pepper.
2. Heat oil in a frying pan over medium heat.
3. Spoon the mixture into the pan, flattening it down.
4. Cook for 10 minutes, then flip and cook for another 5 minutes until crispy.

Nutritional Info: Calories: 350 | Fat: 15g | Carbs: 45g | Protein: 10g

CLASSIC CORNISH PASTY

Prep: 20 mins | Cook: 40 mins | Serves: 4

Cooking Function: Bake

Ingredients:

UK: 500g shortcrust pastry, 200g beef (cubed), 1 potato (peeled and diced), 1 onion (diced), 1 turnip (diced), salt, pepper, 1 egg (for glazing)

Instructions:

1. Preheat the oven to 200°C (fan).
2. Roll out the pastry and cut into large circles.
3. In a bowl, mix the beef, potato, onion, turnip, salt, and pepper.
4. Spoon filling onto one half of the pastry, fold over and crimp the edges.
5. Brush with beaten egg and bake for 30 minutes until golden.

Nutritional Info: Calories: 550 | Fat: 30g | Carbs: 50g | Protein: 25g

PROPER YORKSHIRE PUDDINGS

Prep: 10 mins | Cook: 30 mins | Serves: 4

Cooking Function: Bake

Ingredients:

UK: 140g plain flour, 4 eggs, 200ml milk, 1 teaspoon salt, 100ml vegetable oil

Instructions:

1. Preheat the oven to 220°C (fan).
2. In a bowl, whisk together the flour, eggs, milk, and salt until smooth.
3. Pour oil into a muffin tin and heat in the oven for 5 minutes.
4. Pour the batter into the hot oil, filling each tin halfway.
5. Bake for 20 minutes until puffed and golden.

Nutritional Info: Calories: 300 | Fat: 20g | Carbs: 25g | Protein: 10g

CHAPTER 5: VEGETARIAN VITTLES

MUSHROOM STROGANOFF

Prep: 10 mins | Cook: 20 mins | Serves: 4
Cooking Function: Sauté
Ingredients:

UK: 400g mushrooms (sliced), 1 onion (diced), 2 cloves garlic (minced), 200ml vegetable stock, 150ml sour cream, 2 teaspoons Dijon mustard, 1 teaspoon paprika, 200g pasta, salt, pepper, 30ml olive oil

Instructions:

1. Cook the pasta according to package instructions, then drain and set aside.
2. In a large pan, heat the olive oil over medium heat.
3. Add the diced onion and minced garlic; sauté for 3-4 minutes until softened.
4. Stir in the sliced mushrooms and cook for about 5 minutes until they release their juices.
5. Add the vegetable stock, Dijon mustard, paprika, salt, and pepper. Let it simmer for 5 minutes.
6. Stir in the sour cream until well combined.
7. Toss the cooked pasta into the sauce and mix thoroughly. Serve hot.

Nutritional Info: Calories: 450 | Fat: 15g | Carbs: 55g | Protein: 15g

SWEET POTATO CURRY

Prep: 15 mins | Cook: 30 mins | Serves: 4
Cooking Function: Stew
Ingredients:

UK: 500g sweet potatoes (peeled and cubed), 1 onion (diced), 2 cloves garlic (minced), 1 tablespoon ginger (grated), 400ml coconut milk, 1 can chickpeas (drained), 2 tablespoons curry powder, 1 tablespoon vegetable oil, salt, pepper, coriander (for garnish)

Instructions:

1. In a large pot, heat the vegetable oil over medium heat.
2. Add the diced onion, minced garlic, and grated ginger; sauté for 5 minutes until soft.
3. Stir in the curry powder and cook for another minute until fragrant.
4. Add the cubed sweet potatoes and coconut milk, bringing to a simmer.
5. Cook for 15-20 minutes until the sweet potatoes are tender.
6. Stir in the chickpeas and cook for an additional 5 minutes.
7. Season with salt and pepper, and garnish with coriander before serving.

Nutritional Info: Calories: 400 | Fat: 18g | Carbs: 50g | Protein: 10g

VEGGIE CHILLI

Prep: 10 mins | Cook: 40 mins | Serves: 4

Cooking Function: Stew

Ingredients:

UK: 1 can kidney beans (drained), 1 can black beans (drained), 1 can chopped tomatoes, 1 bell pepper (diced), 1 onion (diced), 2 cloves garlic (minced), 2 teaspoons chilli powder, 1 tablespoon olive oil, salt, pepper, 150ml vegetable stock

Instructions:

1. Heat the olive oil in a large pot over medium heat.
2. Add the diced onion and garlic; sauté for 5 minutes until soft.
3. Stir in the diced bell pepper and cook for another 3 minutes.
4. Add the chilli powder, kidney beans, black beans, chopped tomatoes, and vegetable stock.
5. Bring to a boil, then reduce the heat and simmer for 30 minutes.
6. Season with salt and pepper before serving hot.

Nutritional Info: Calories: 350 | Fat: 5g | Carbs: 60g | Protein: 20g

HALLOUMI STIR FRY

Prep: 10 mins | **Cook:** 15 mins | **Serves:** 2

Cooking Function: Sauté

Ingredients:

UK: 250g halloumi (sliced), 1 courgette (sliced), 1 bell pepper (sliced), 1 red onion (sliced), 2 tablespoons soy sauce, 30ml olive oil, salt, pepper, 1 teaspoon sesame seeds (for garnish)

Instructions:

1. In a large frying pan, heat the olive oil over medium-high heat.
2. Add the sliced red onion and bell pepper; sauté for 3 minutes.
3. Stir in the courgette and cook for another 5 minutes until tender.
4. Add the halloumi slices and soy sauce, cooking until the halloumi is golden brown.
5. Season with salt and pepper, then sprinkle with sesame seeds before serving.

Nutritional Info: Calories: 500 | Fat: 35g | Carbs: 25g | Protein: 25g

VEGETABLE LASAGNE

Prep: 20 mins | **Cook:** 45 mins | **Serves:** 4

Cooking Function: Bake

Ingredients:

UK: 9 lasagne sheets, 400g spinach, 200g ricotta cheese, 200g mozzarella (sliced), 400g passata, 1 onion (diced), 1 carrot (grated), 1 zucchini (grated), 2 cloves garlic (minced), 30ml olive oil, salt, pepper

Instructions:

1. Preheat the oven to 180°C (fan).
2. In a frying pan, heat the olive oil over medium heat.
3. Add the onion and garlic; sauté for 5 minutes until soft.
4. Stir in the grated carrot and zucchini, cooking for another 5 minutes.
5. Add the spinach until wilted, then season with salt and pepper.
6. In a baking dish, layer the passata, lasagne sheets, ricotta mixture (spinach, onion mix), and mozzarella. Repeat until ingredients are used up, finishing with mozzarella on top.
7. Bake for 30 minutes until golden and bubbly.

Nutritional Info: Calories: 600 | Fat: 25g | Carbs: 60g | Protein: 30g

MUSHROOM RISOTTO

Prep: 10 mins | Cook: 30 mins | Serves: 4

Cooking Function: Sauté

Ingredients:

UK: 300g Arborio rice, 400g mushrooms (sliced), 1 onion (diced), 2 cloves garlic (minced), 1L vegetable stock, 100ml white wine (optional), 50g parmesan cheese (grated), 30ml olive oil, salt, pepper, parsley (for garnish)

Instructions:

1. In a saucepan, heat the vegetable stock and keep it warm.
2. In a large pan, heat the olive oil over medium heat.
3. Add the onion and garlic; sauté for 5 minutes until soft.
4. Stir in the sliced mushrooms and cook until tender.
5. Add the Arborio rice, stirring for 1-2 minutes until slightly translucent.
6. Pour in the white wine (if using) and stir until absorbed.
7. Gradually add the warm vegetable stock, one ladle at a time, stirring continuously until absorbed before adding more.
8. Once the rice is creamy and al dente, stir in the parmesan cheese and season with salt and pepper. Garnish with parsley before serving.

Nutritional Info: Calories: 500 | Fat: 15g | Carbs: 75g | Protein: 15g

BEAN BURGERS

Prep: 10 mins | Cook: 20 mins | Serves: 4

Cooking Function: Fry

Ingredients:

UK: 400g canned beans (mixed), 1 onion (diced), 1 teaspoon cumin, 100g breadcrumbs, 1 egg, salt, pepper, 30ml olive oil

Instructions:

1. In a bowl, mash the mixed beans with a fork.
2. Stir in the diced onion, cumin, breadcrumbs, egg, salt, and pepper until well combined.
3. Shape the mixture into patties.
4. In a frying pan, heat the olive oil over medium heat.
5. Fry the patties for about 5 minutes on each side until golden brown. Serve in buns with your favourite toppings.

Nutritional Info: Calories: 350 | Fat: 10g | Carbs: 50g | Protein: 15g

VEGETABLE FAJITAS

Prep: 10 mins | Cook: 15 mins | Serves: 4

Cooking Function: Sauté

Ingredients:

UK: 1 bell pepper (sliced), 1 courgette (sliced), 1 onion (sliced), 2 teaspoons fajita seasoning, 30ml olive oil, tortillas (to serve), salt, pepper

Instructions:

1. In a large frying pan, heat the olive oil over medium heat.
2. Add the sliced onion, bell pepper, and courgette; sauté for 5 minutes.
3. Stir in the fajita seasoning, salt, and pepper, cooking for another 5-7 minutes until the veggies are tender.
4. Serve the fajita mixture in warmed tortillas.

Nutritional Info: Calories: 300 | Fat: 10g | Carbs: 40g | Protein: 10g

CAULIFLOWER MAC AND CHEESE

Prep: 15 mins | Cook: 30 mins | Serves: 4

Cooking Function: Bake

Ingredients:

UK: 400g cauliflower florets, 200g macaroni, 150g cheddar cheese (grated), 200ml milk, 30g butter, 30g flour, salt, pepper

Instructions:

1. Preheat the oven to 180°C (fan).
2. Cook the macaroni according to package instructions.
3. Steam the cauliflower florets until tender.
4. In a saucepan, melt the butter over medium heat.
5. Stir in the flour to make a roux, then gradually add the milk, stirring until thickened.
6. Add the grated cheddar, salt, and pepper until melted.
7. Mix the cooked macaroni and cauliflower into the cheese sauce.
8. Transfer to a baking dish and bake for 20 minutes until golden.

Nutritional Info: Calories: 550 | Fat: 25g | Carbs: 60g | Protein: 20g

SPINACH AND CHICKPEA CURRY

Prep: 10 mins | Cook: 25 mins | Serves: 4

Cooking Function: Stew

Ingredients:

UK: 400g spinach, 1 can chickpeas (drained), 1 onion (diced), 2 cloves garlic (minced), 1 tablespoon curry powder, 400ml coconut milk, 30ml olive oil, salt, pepper

Instructions:

1. In a large pot, heat the olive oil over medium heat.
2. Add the diced onion and garlic; sauté for 5 minutes until soft.
3. Stir in the curry powder and cook for another minute.
4. Add the chickpeas and coconut milk, bringing to a simmer.
5. Stir in the spinach until wilted. Season with salt and pepper before serving.

Nutritional Info: Calories: 350 | Fat: 20g | Carbs: 30g | Protein: 15g

VEGETABLE SHEPHERD'S PIE

Prep: 15 mins | Cook: 45 mins | Serves: 4

Cooking Function: Bake

Ingredients:

UK: 400g mixed vegetables (carrots, peas, corn), 500g potatoes (peeled and cubed), 100ml vegetable stock, 1 tablespoon tomato puree, 1 tablespoon olive oil, salt, pepper

Instructions:

1. Preheat the oven to 200°C (fan).
2. Boil the potatoes until tender, then mash with salt and pepper.
3. In a pan, heat the olive oil and add the mixed vegetables; sauté for 5 minutes.
4. Stir in the vegetable stock and tomato puree, cooking for another 5 minutes.
5. Spread the vegetable mixture in a baking dish and top with mashed potatoes.
6. Bake for 20 minutes until golden on top.

Nutritional Info: Calories: 450 | Fat: 10g | Carbs: 70g | Protein: 15g

BUDDHA BOWL

Prep: 10 mins | Cook: 20 mins | Serves: 2

Cooking Function: Steam

Ingredients:

UK: 200g quinoa, 1 avocado (sliced), 100g cherry tomatoes (halved), 1 carrot (grated), 200g spinach, 30ml olive oil, 1 lemon (juiced), salt, pepper

Instructions:

1. Cook the quinoa according to package instructions and set aside.
2. In a bowl, combine the spinach, avocado, cherry tomatoes, and grated carrot.
3. Drizzle with olive oil and lemon juice; season with salt and pepper.
4. Serve the vegetable mixture over a bed of quinoa.

Nutritional Info: Calories: 400 | Fat: 20g | Carbs: 40g | Protein: 10g

STUFFED PEPPERS

Prep: 15 mins | Cook: 30 mins | Serves: 4

Cooking Function: Bake

Ingredients:

UK: 4 bell peppers (halved), 200g quinoa (cooked), 1 can black beans (drained), 1 onion (diced), 1 teaspoon cumin, 150g cheese (grated), salt, pepper

Instructions:

1. Preheat the oven to 190°C (fan).

2. In a bowl, mix the cooked quinoa, black beans, diced onion, cumin, salt, and pepper.

3. Stuff the mixture into the halved bell peppers and top with cheese.

4. Place in a baking dish and bake for 30 minutes until the peppers are tender.

Nutritional Info: Calories: 350 | Fat: 15g | Carbs: 40g | Protein: 15g

CHAPTER 6: 15-MIN AIR FRYER MAGIC

PERFECT CHICKEN BREAST

Prep: 5 mins | Cook: 15 mins | Serves: 2
Cooking Function: Air Fry
Ingredients:

UK: 2 chicken breasts, 30ml olive oil, 1 teaspoon garlic powder, 1 teaspoon smoked paprika, salt, pepper

Instructions:

1. Preheat the air fryer to 200°C (fan).
2. In a bowl, coat the chicken breasts with olive oil, garlic powder, smoked paprika, salt, and pepper.
3. Place the seasoned chicken in the air fryer basket, ensuring they are not touching.
4. Cook for 15 minutes, flipping halfway through, until the chicken is cooked through and golden brown.
5. Let them rest for a few minutes before slicing. Enjoy your juicy chicken breast with a side salad or in a wrap!

Nutritional Info: Calories: 300 | Fat: 12g | Carbs: 1g | Protein: 44g

CRISPY SALMON

Prep: 5 mins | Cook: 10 mins | Serves: 2
Cooking Function: Air Fry
Ingredients:

UK: 2 salmon fillets, 30ml olive oil, 1 tablespoon soy sauce, 1 teaspoon lemon juice, salt, pepper

Instructions:

1. Preheat the air fryer to 200°C (fan).
2. In a small bowl, whisk together olive oil, soy sauce, lemon juice, salt, and pepper.
3. Brush the mixture over the salmon fillets.
4. Place the salmon in the air fryer basket, skin-side down.
5. Cook for 10 minutes until the salmon is flaky and slightly crispy. Serve with steamed veggies for a quick, healthy meal!

Nutritional Info: Calories: 280 | Fat: 20g | Carbs: 2g | Protein: 23g

PORK CHOPS

Prep: 5 mins | Cook: 15 mins | Serves: 2
Cooking Function: Air Fry
Ingredients:
UK: 2 pork chops, 30ml olive oil, 1 teaspoon garlic powder, 1 teaspoon dried thyme, salt, pepper
Instructions:
1. Preheat the air fryer to 200°C (fan).
2. Rub the pork chops with olive oil, garlic powder, thyme, salt, and pepper.
3. Place the pork chops in the air fryer basket in a single layer.
4. Cook for 15 minutes, flipping halfway through until they reach an internal temperature of 70°C.
5. Let them rest for a few minutes before digging in. They're perfect with mashed potatoes!
Nutritional Info: Calories: 350 | Fat: 22g | Carbs: 1g | Protein: 32g

LAMB KOFTAS

Prep: 10 mins | Cook: 12 mins | Serves: 4
Cooking Function: Air Fry
Ingredients:
UK: 500g minced lamb, 1 onion (finely chopped), 2 cloves garlic (minced), 1 teaspoon cumin, 1 teaspoon coriander, salt, pepper, skewers
Instructions:
1. Preheat the air fryer to 200°C (fan).
2. In a bowl, mix the minced lamb, onion, garlic, cumin, coriander, salt, and pepper.
3. Shape the mixture into kofta shapes and thread them onto skewers.
4. Place the koftas in the air fryer basket.
5. Cook for 12 minutes, turning halfway, until browned and cooked through. Serve with tzatziki and pita for a tasty meal!
Nutritional Info: Calories: 400 | Fat: 30g | Carbs: 5g | Protein: 30g

BEEF STEAK

Prep: 5 mins | Cook: 10 mins | Serves: 2
Cooking Function: Air Fry
Ingredients:
UK: 2 beef steaks, 30ml olive oil, salt, pepper, 1 teaspoon rosemary (optional)
Instructions:
1. Preheat the air fryer to 200°C (fan).
2. Rub the steaks with olive oil, salt, pepper, and rosemary.
3. Place the steaks in the air fryer basket.
4. Cook for 10 minutes for medium-rare, flipping halfway through. Adjust the time for your preferred doneness.
5. Let them rest for a couple of minutes before serving. Perfect with chips or a salad!
Nutritional Info: Calories: 400 | Fat: 20g | Carbs: 0g | Protein: 50g

CRISPY PRAWNS

Prep: 10 mins | Cook: 8 mins | Serves: 2
Cooking Function: Air Fry
Ingredients:
UK: 250g prawns (peeled), 50g breadcrumbs, 30ml olive oil, 1 teaspoon paprika, salt, pepper
Instructions:
1. Preheat the air fryer to 200°C (fan).
2. In a bowl, toss the prawns with olive oil, paprika, salt, and pepper.
3. Coat them in breadcrumbs until fully covered.
4. Place the prawns in a single layer in the air fryer basket.
5. Cook for 8 minutes, shaking halfway, until crispy. Serve with sweet chilli sauce for a fun snack!
Nutritional Info: Calories: 250 | Fat: 10g | Carbs: 15g | Protein: 25g

CHINESE-STYLE WINGS

Prep: 10 mins | Cook: 25 mins | Serves: 4

Cooking Function: Air Fry

Ingredients:

UK: 800g chicken wings, 30ml soy sauce, 30ml honey, 1 tablespoon sesame oil, 1 teaspoon five-spice powder, salt, pepper

Instructions:

1. Preheat the air fryer to 200°C (fan).
2. In a bowl, mix the soy sauce, honey, sesame oil, five-spice powder, salt, and pepper.
3. Add the chicken wings and toss until well-coated.
4. Place the wings in the air fryer basket in a single layer.
5. Cook for 25 minutes, shaking halfway, until they're crispy and cooked through. Serve with a side of rice or salad!

Nutritional Info: Calories: 400 | Fat: 25g | Carbs: 15g | Protein: 30g

AIR FRIED SCHNITZEL

Prep: 10 mins | Cook: 15 mins | Serves: 2

Cooking Function: Air Fry

Ingredients:

UK: 2 chicken breasts (flattened), 50g flour, 1 egg (beaten), 100g breadcrumbs, 30ml olive oil, salt, pepper

Instructions:

1. Preheat the air fryer to 200°C (fan).
2. Set up a breading station: one plate with flour, one with beaten egg, and one with breadcrumbs mixed with salt and pepper.
3. Coat each chicken breast in flour, dip in egg, then coat with breadcrumbs.
4. Drizzle olive oil over the schnitzels.
5. Place them in the air fryer basket and cook for 15 minutes, flipping halfway through. Serve with lemon wedges!

Nutritional Info: Calories: 400 | Fat: 18g | Carbs: 35g | Protein: 32g

SEASONED CHICKEN THIGHS

Prep: 5 mins | Cook: 20 mins | Serves: 4

Cooking Function: Air Fry

Ingredients:

UK: 4 chicken thighs (skin-on), 30ml olive oil, 1 teaspoon paprika, 1 teaspoon garlic powder, salt, pepper

Instructions:

1. Preheat the air fryer to 200°C (fan).
2. Rub the chicken thighs with olive oil, paprika, garlic powder, salt, and pepper.
3. Place the thighs skin-side up in the air fryer basket.
4. Cook for 20 minutes, flipping halfway, until the skin is crispy and the chicken is cooked through. Serve with rice and veggies!

Nutritional Info: Calories: 320 | Fat: 24g | Carbs: 0g | Protein: 28g

FISH AND CHIPS

Prep: 10 mins | Cook: 25 mins | Serves: 2

Cooking Function: Air Fry

Ingredients:

UK: 2 white fish fillets (like cod), 100g breadcrumbs, 30ml flour, 1 egg (beaten), 300g frozen chips, 30ml olive oil, salt, pepper

Instructions:

1. Preheat the air fryer to 200°C (fan).
2. Set up a breading station: one plate with flour, one with beaten egg, and one with breadcrumbs seasoned with salt and pepper.
3. Coat each fish fillet in flour, dip in egg, then coat with breadcrumbs.
4. Place the frozen chips in the air fryer basket and drizzle with olive oil.
5. Add the breaded fish on top and cook for 25 minutes, shaking halfway, until crispy and golden. Serve with tartar sauce!

Nutritional Info: Calories: 600 | Fat: 30g | Carbs: 50g | Protein: 30g

CRISPY TOFU

Prep: 10 mins | Cook: 15 mins | Serves: 2

Cooking Function: Air Fry

Ingredients:

UK: 300g firm tofu (pressed and cubed), 30ml soy sauce, 1 tablespoon cornstarch, 30ml olive oil, salt, pepper

Instructions:

1. Preheat the air fryer to 200°C (fan).

2. In a bowl, toss the cubed tofu with soy sauce, cornstarch, olive oil, salt, and pepper until evenly coated.

3. Place the tofu cubes in a single layer in the air fryer basket.

4. Cook for 15 minutes, shaking halfway, until crispy. Serve with stir-fried veggies or rice for a satisfying meal!

Nutritional Info: Calories: 250 | Fat: 16g | Carbs: 10g | Protein: 22g

BBQ RIBS

Prep: 10 mins | Cook: 25 mins | Serves: 2

Cooking Function: Air Fry

Ingredients:

UK: 500g pork ribs, 50ml BBQ sauce, salt, pepper

Instructions:

1. Preheat the air fryer to 200°C (fan).
2. Season the ribs with salt and pepper.
3. Brush the BBQ sauce over the ribs until well coated.
4. Place the ribs in the air fryer basket.
5. Cook for 25 minutes, flipping halfway, until they're tender and caramelized. Serve with coleslaw for a great meal!

Nutritional Info: Calories: 450 | Fat: 30g | Carbs: 10g | Protein: 35g

CHICKEN KATSU

Prep: 10 mins | Cook: 15 mins | Serves: 2

Cooking Function: Air Fry

Ingredients:

UK: 2 chicken breasts, 50g flour, 1 egg (beaten), 100g panko breadcrumbs, 30ml olive oil, salt, pepper

Instructions:

1. Preheat the air fryer to 200°C (fan).

2. Set up a breading station: one plate with flour, one with beaten egg, and one with panko breadcrumbs mixed with salt and pepper.

3. Coat each chicken breast in flour, dip in egg, then coat with panko breadcrumbs.

4. Drizzle olive oil over the breaded chicken.

5. Place them in the air fryer basket and cook for 15 minutes, flipping halfway. Serve with tonkatsu sauce and rice!

Nutritional Info: Calories: 450 | Fat: 20g | Carbs: 35g | Protein: 36g

CHAPTER 7: FRIENDS AROUND

NACHOS PARTY PLATTER

Prep: 10 mins | Cook: 10 mins | Serves: 4

Cooking Function: Air Fry

Ingredients:

UK: 200g tortilla chips, 150g grated cheese (cheddar or Monterey Jack), 100g cooked chicken (shredded), 50g jalapeños (sliced), 100g salsa, 100g sour cream, fresh coriander (for garnish)

Instructions:

1. Preheat the air fryer to 180°C (fan).
2. Layer half of the tortilla chips in the air fryer basket.
3. Sprinkle half of the grated cheese, shredded chicken, and jalapeños over the chips.
4. Repeat the layers with the remaining chips and toppings.
5. Cook for 8-10 minutes, until the cheese is melted and bubbly.
6. Carefully remove the nachos from the air fryer and transfer them to a serving platter.
7. Serve with salsa, sour cream, and a sprinkle of fresh coriander for a fun and tasty sharing platter!

Nutritional Info: Calories: 350 | Fat: 20g | Carbs: 30g | Protein: 15g

BUILD-YOUR-OWN TACO BAR

Prep: 15 mins | Cook: 20 mins | Serves: 6

Cooking Function: Grill

Ingredients:

UK: 500g minced beef (or turkey), 1 onion (diced), 2 cloves garlic (minced), 2 tablespoons taco seasoning, 12 taco shells, 150g grated cheese, 100g lettuce (shredded), 100g tomatoes (diced), 100g salsa, 100g guacamole

Instructions:

1. Preheat the grill to medium heat.
2. In a skillet, cook the diced onion and minced garlic until soft.
3. Add the minced beef and taco seasoning; cook until browned and fully cooked.
4. While the beef cooks, warm the taco shells on the grill for about 2 minutes.
5. Set up a taco bar with cooked beef, taco shells, cheese, lettuce, tomatoes, salsa, and guacamole.
6. Let everyone build their tacos with their favourite toppings for a personalised feast!

Nutritional Info: Calories: 500 | Fat: 25g | Carbs: 40g | Protein: 30g

SHARING PIZZAS

Prep: 15 mins | Cook: 15 mins | Serves: 4

Cooking Function: Air Fry

Ingredients:

UK: 2 pizza bases, 200g pizza sauce, 200g grated cheese, 100g pepperoni slices, 100g mushrooms (sliced), 50g olives, 1 teaspoon dried oregano

Instructions:

1. Preheat the air fryer to 200°C (fan).
2. Spread a generous layer of pizza sauce over each pizza base.
3. Sprinkle the grated cheese evenly over the sauce.
4. Add your choice of toppings: pepperoni, mushrooms, olives, and a sprinkle of oregano.
5. Place the pizzas in the air fryer basket and cook for 12-15 minutes, or until the cheese is melted and bubbly.
6. Slice and share for a delightful pizza night with friends!

Nutritional Info: Calories: 400 | Fat: 22g | Carbs: 36g | Protein: 18g

PARTY CHICKEN WINGS

Prep: 10 mins | Cook: 25 mins | Serves: 4

Cooking Function: Air Fry

Ingredients:

UK: 1kg chicken wings, 50ml BBQ sauce, 50ml hot sauce, 1 tablespoon garlic powder, salt, pepper

Instructions:

1. Preheat the air fryer to 200°C (fan).
2. In a bowl, toss the chicken wings with BBQ sauce, hot sauce, garlic powder, salt, and pepper until well coated.
3. Arrange the wings in a single layer in the air fryer basket.
4. Cook for 25 minutes, shaking halfway, until crispy and cooked through.
5. Serve the wings with extra sauce on the side for dipping. Perfect for game nights!

Nutritional Info: Calories: 500 | Fat: 30g | Carbs: 10g | Protein: 45g

LOADING GAMING NIGHT SNACKS

Prep: 10 mins | Cook: 10 mins | Serves: 4
Cooking Function: Air Fry
Ingredients:

UK: 250g mini sausages, 150g mozzarella sticks, 200g potato wedges, 50g BBQ sauce, 50g sweet chilli sauce

Instructions:

1. Preheat the air fryer to 200°C (fan).
2. Place the mini sausages and potato wedges in the air fryer basket.
3. Cook for 8 minutes, then add the mozzarella sticks to the basket.
4. Cook for another 2-3 minutes until everything is golden and crispy.
5. Serve with BBQ and sweet chilli sauces for dipping. Ideal for snacking while gaming!

Nutritional Info: Calories: 450 | Fat: 30g | Carbs: 35g | Protein: 20g

MOVIE NIGHT FEAST

Prep: 15 mins | Cook: 15 mins | Serves: 4
Cooking Function: Air Fry
Ingredients:

UK: 200g popcorn kernels, 30ml vegetable oil, 100g chocolate buttons, 100g marshmallows, 50g nuts (optional)

Instructions:

1. Preheat the air fryer to 180°C (fan).
2. In a bowl, toss the popcorn kernels with vegetable oil.
3. Place the kernels in the air fryer basket and cook for about 8-10 minutes until popped.
4. Once popped, transfer the popcorn to a large bowl and mix in chocolate buttons, marshmallows, and nuts if using.
5. Enjoy this sweet and crunchy treat while watching your favourite films!

Nutritional Info: Calories: 400 | Fat: 18g | Carbs: 50g | Protein: 6g

STUDENT PARTY PUNCH

Prep: 5 mins | Cook: 0 mins | Serves: 6
Cooking Function: None
Ingredients:

UK: 500ml lemonade, 500ml fruit punch, 250ml orange juice, 250g mixed fruit (frozen or fresh), mint leaves (for garnish)

Instructions:

1. In a large jug, combine the lemonade, fruit punch, and orange juice.
2. Add the mixed fruit and stir well.
3. Chill in the fridge for about 30 minutes to let the flavours mingle.
4. Serve in glasses with fresh mint leaves for a refreshing party drink!

Nutritional Info: Calories: 150 | Fat: 0g | Carbs: 37g | Protein: 1g

SHARING PLATTER

Prep: 10 mins | Cook: 0 mins | Serves: 4
Cooking Function: None
Ingredients:

UK: 100g hummus, 100g tzatziki, 200g mixed vegetable sticks (carrots, cucumber, peppers), 150g olives, 100g cheese cubes

Instructions:

1. On a large serving platter, arrange the hummus and tzatziki in bowls.
2. Neatly place the vegetable sticks, olives, and cheese cubes around the dips.
3. Serve with pita bread or crackers for a delicious and healthy sharing platter!

Nutritional Info: Calories: 300 | Fat: 15g | Carbs: 30g | Protein: 10g

GIANT COOKIE PIZZA

Prep: 15 mins | Cook: 12 mins | Serves: 8

Cooking Function: Air Fry

Ingredients:

UK: 150g butter (softened), 150g brown sugar, 100g caster sugar, 1 egg, 1 teaspoon vanilla extract, 300g plain flour, 100g chocolate chips

Instructions:

1. Preheat the air fryer to 180°C (fan).
2. In a bowl, cream together the softened butter, brown sugar, and caster sugar until fluffy.
3. Add the egg and vanilla extract; mix until combined.
4. Gradually add the flour and chocolate chips; mix until a dough forms.
5. Press the dough into the air fryer basket to form a large pizza shape.
6. Cook for 12 minutes, until golden brown. Let cool, then slice into wedges for a fun dessert!

Nutritional Info: Calories: 250 | Fat: 12g | Carbs: 30g | Protein: 3g

PASTA PARTY

Prep: 15 mins | Cook: 20 mins | Serves: 4

Cooking Function: Boil

Ingredients:

UK: 300g pasta (your choice), 200g cherry tomatoes (halved), 100g spinach, 50g parmesan cheese (grated), 30ml olive oil, salt, pepper

Instructions:

1. Cook the pasta in boiling salted water according to package instructions until al dente.
2. In a separate pan, heat the olive oil and add the cherry tomatoes; sauté for 5 minutes until soft.
3. Stir in the spinach until wilted, then combine with the drained pasta.
4. Season with salt and pepper, and sprinkle with parmesan cheese before serving for a delightful pasta party!

Nutritional Info: Calories: 400 | Fat: 15g | Carbs: 50g | Protein: 12g

DIY BURGER BAR

Prep: 20 mins | Cook: 10 mins | Serves: 4

Cooking Function: Grill

Ingredients:

UK: 500g minced beef, 1 teaspoon salt, 1 teaspoon pepper, 4 burger buns, 100g lettuce, 100g tomatoes (sliced), 100g cheese slices, ketchup, mustard

Instructions:

1. Preheat the grill to medium-high.

2. In a bowl, season the minced beef with salt and pepper; form into 4 burger patties.

3. Grill the patties for about 5 minutes on each side, or until cooked to your liking.

4. Toast the burger buns on the grill for 1-2 minutes.

5. Set up a DIY burger bar with all the toppings: lettuce, tomatoes, cheese, ketchup, and mustard for a fun and interactive meal!

Nutritional Info: Calories: 500 | Fat: 28g | Carbs: 40g | Protein: 30g

MATCH DAY SNACKS

Prep: 10 mins | Cook: 15 mins | Serves: 4

Cooking Function: Air Fry

Ingredients:

UK: 200g potato wedges, 100g mozzarella sticks, 100g chicken nuggets, 50g BBQ sauce (for dipping)

Instructions:

1. Preheat the air fryer to 200°C (fan).
2. Place the potato wedges, mozzarella sticks, and chicken nuggets in the air fryer basket.
3. Cook for 15 minutes, shaking halfway through for even cooking.
4. Serve hot with BBQ sauce for dipping while cheering on your team!

Nutritional Info: Calories: 400 | Fat: 25g | Carbs: 30g | Protein: 15g

MOVIE NIGHT POPCORN BAR

Prep: 10 mins | Cook: 10 mins | Serves: 6
Cooking Function: Air Fry
Ingredients:

UK: 100g popcorn kernels, 30ml vegetable oil, 50g butter (melted), assorted toppings (salt, cheese powder, caramel sauce, chocolate drizzle)

Instructions:

1. Preheat the air fryer to 180°C (fan).
2. Toss the popcorn kernels with vegetable oil and place them in the air fryer basket.
3. Cook for about 8-10 minutes, until popped.
4. Transfer the popcorn to a large bowl and drizzle with melted butter.
5. Set up a toppings station for everyone to customise their popcorn for a fun movie night treat!

Nutritional Info: Calories: 300 | Fat: 15g | Carbs: 35g | Protein: 5g

CHAPTER 8: DATE NIGHT SPECIALS

STEAK WITH PEPPERCORN SAUCE

Prep: 10 mins | Cook: 15 mins | Serves: 2

Cooking Function: Fry

Ingredients:

UK: 2 ribeye steaks (about 200g each), 2 tablespoons olive oil, salt and pepper (to taste), 100ml beef stock, 2 tablespoons green peppercorns, 50ml double cream, 1 tablespoon Dijon mustard

Instructions:

1. Heat the olive oil in a frying pan over medium-high heat.
2. Season the steaks with salt and pepper, then sear them in the hot pan for about 4-5 minutes on each side, depending on your preferred doneness.
3. Remove the steaks and let them rest while you make the sauce.
4. In the same pan, add the beef stock and bring it to a boil, scraping up any browned bits from the bottom.
5. Stir in the green peppercorns, double cream, and Dijon mustard, and simmer for a couple of minutes until slightly thickened.
6. Serve the steaks topped with the peppercorn sauce. Enjoy a lovely dinner that impresses without the fuss!

Nutritional Info: Calories: 500 | Fat: 35g | Carbs: 5g | Protein: 40g

CREAMY GARLIC PRAWNS

Prep: 5 mins | Cook: 10 mins | Serves: 2

Cooking Function: Sauté

Ingredients:

UK: 200g raw prawns (peeled and deveined), 2 tablespoons olive oil, 3 garlic cloves (minced), 100ml double cream, 50g grated parmesan, salt and pepper (to taste), 1 tablespoon chopped fresh parsley

Instructions:
1. Heat olive oil in a pan over medium heat.
2. Add minced garlic and sauté for about 1 minute until fragrant (be careful not to burn it!).
3. Toss in the prawns and cook for 2-3 minutes until they turn pink.
4. Pour in the double cream and parmesan, stirring until the sauce thickens slightly.
5. Season with salt and pepper, then garnish with chopped parsley before serving. Pair it with crusty bread for a delicious treat!

Nutritional Info: Calories: 450 | Fat: 35g | Carbs: 5g | Protein: 30g

HOMEMADE PASTA

Prep: 15 mins | Cook: 2 mins | Serves: 2

Cooking Function: Boil

Ingredients:

UK: 200g plain flour, 2 large eggs, a pinch of salt, 1 tablespoon olive oil

Instructions:
1. In a bowl, mix the flour and salt, then make a well in the centre.
2. Crack the eggs into the well and add olive oil. Using a fork, slowly combine the flour with the eggs until it forms a dough.
3. Knead the dough for about 5 minutes until smooth, then cover and let it rest for 30 minutes.
4. Roll out the dough thinly and cut it into your desired pasta shape.
5. Boil in salted water for 2 minutes until cooked, then drain. Serve with your favourite sauce!

Nutritional Info: Calories: 350 | Fat: 10g | Carbs: 50g | Protein: 12g

ROMANTIC RISOTTO

Prep: 5 mins | Cook: 30 mins | Serves: 2
Cooking Function: Sauté
Ingredients:

UK: 150g Arborio rice, 1 small onion (finely chopped), 2 garlic cloves (minced), 600ml vegetable stock, 50ml white wine, 50g grated parmesan, 2 tablespoons olive oil, salt and pepper (to taste), 50g peas

Instructions:

1. Heat the olive oil in a pan over medium heat and sauté the onion and garlic for 2-3 minutes until softened.
2. Add the Arborio rice and stir for 1-2 minutes to coat it in oil.
3. Pour in the white wine and let it absorb.
4. Gradually add the vegetable stock, one ladle at a time, stirring until absorbed before adding more.
5. After about 20 minutes, stir in the peas and cook until the rice is creamy and al dente.
6. Finish with parmesan, salt, and pepper. Serve warm for a comforting, romantic meal!

Nutritional Info: Calories: 400 | Fat: 10g | Carbs: 65g | Protein: 15g

PAN-SEARED SALMON

Prep: 5 mins | Cook: 10 mins | Serves: 2
Cooking Function: Fry
Ingredients:

UK: 2 salmon fillets (about 150g each), 1 tablespoon olive oil, salt and pepper (to taste), 1 lemon (sliced), fresh dill (for garnish)

Instructions:

1. Heat the olive oil in a frying pan over medium-high heat.
2. Season the salmon fillets with salt and pepper, then place them upside down in the pan.
3. Cook for 4-5 minutes, then flip and cook for another 2-3 minutes until cooked through.
4. Serve with lemon slices and fresh dill for a simple yet elegant dish!

Nutritional Info: Calories: 350 | Fat: 25g | Carbs: 2g | Protein: 30g

CHICKEN KIEV

Prep: 15 mins | Cook: 20 mins | Serves: 2
Cooking Function: Bake
Ingredients:

UK: 2 chicken breasts, 50g unsalted butter (softened), 2 cloves garlic (minced), 1 tablespoon fresh parsley (chopped), 100g breadcrumbs, 1 egg (beaten), salt and pepper (to taste)

Instructions:

1. Preheat the oven to 200°C (fan).
2. In a bowl, mix the softened butter, garlic, parsley, salt, and pepper.
3. Carefully cut a pocket into each chicken breast and stuff with the garlic butter mixture.
4. Dip each stuffed chicken breast in the beaten egg, then coat in breadcrumbs.
5. Bake in the oven for 20 minutes until golden and cooked through. Enjoy with a side salad or chips!

Nutritional Info: Calories: 600 | Fat: 35g | Carbs: 30g | Protein: 40g

MUSHROOM TAGLIATELLE

Prep: 10 mins | Cook: 15 mins | Serves: 2
Cooking Function: Boil and Sauté
Ingredients:

UK: 200g tagliatelle, 200g mushrooms (sliced), 2 garlic cloves (minced), 100ml double cream, 30g grated parmesan, 1 tablespoon olive oil, salt and pepper (to taste), fresh parsley (for garnish)

Instructions:

1. Cook the tagliatelle in boiling salted water according to the package instructions.
2. In a pan, heat olive oil and sauté the garlic and mushrooms for about 5 minutes until softened.
3. Stir in the double cream and let it simmer for a few minutes until thickened.
4. Combine the drained pasta with the sauce, adding parmesan, salt, and pepper.
5. Garnish with fresh parsley and serve for a comforting dish!

Nutritional Info: Calories: 500 | Fat: 25g | Carbs: 55g | Protein: 15g

THAI GREEN CURRY

Prep: 10 mins | Cook: 20 mins | Serves: 2

Cooking Function: Simmer

Ingredients:

UK: 200g chicken breast (sliced), 1 tablespoon green curry paste, 400ml coconut milk, 100g mixed vegetables (frozen or fresh), 1 tablespoon fish sauce, 1 tablespoon vegetable oil, fresh basil (for garnish), jasmine rice (to serve)

Instructions:

1. Heat vegetable oil in a pan over medium heat and sauté the chicken until browned.

2. Add the green curry paste and cook for another minute until fragrant.

3. Pour in the coconut milk and bring to a simmer.

4. Add the mixed vegetables and fish sauce, cooking for about 10 minutes until the chicken is cooked through.

5. Serve with jasmine rice and garnish with fresh basil for a taste of Thailand!

Nutritional Info: Calories: 550 | Fat: 35g | Carbs: 30g | Protein: 30g

STUFFED CHICKEN BREAST

Prep: 15 mins | Cook: 25 mins | Serves: 2

Cooking Function: Bake

Ingredients:

UK: 2 chicken breasts, 100g spinach (cooked and chopped), 50g feta cheese, 1 tablespoon olive oil, salt and pepper (to taste)

Instructions:

1. Preheat the oven to 200°C (fan).

2. In a bowl, mix the spinach, feta cheese, salt, and pepper.

3. Carefully cut a pocket in each chicken breast and fill it with the spinach and feta mixture.

4. Brush the outside of the chicken with olive oil and season.

5. Bake for 25 minutes until cooked through. Serve with a side salad or steamed vegetables!

Nutritional Info: Calories: 400 | Fat: 20g | Carbs: 2g | Protein: 50g

MEDITERRANEAN SEA BASS

Prep: 10 mins | Cook: 20 mins | Serves: 2

Cooking Function: Bake

Ingredients:

UK: 2 whole sea bass (cleaned), 1 lemon (sliced), 1 tablespoon olive oil, salt and pepper (to taste), fresh rosemary (for garnish)

Instructions:

1. Preheat the oven to 200°C (fan).
2. Place the sea bass on a baking tray and drizzle with olive oil, seasoning with salt and pepper.
3. Stuff the cavity of each fish with lemon slices and fresh rosemary.
4. Bake for 20 minutes until the fish is cooked through and flaky. Serve with new potatoes or a salad for a healthy dinner!

Nutritional Info: Calories: 350 | Fat: 20g | Carbs: 5g | Protein: 35g

VEGETARIAN WELLINGTON

Prep: 20 mins | Cook: 35 mins | Serves: 2

Cooking Function: Bake

Ingredients:

UK: 250g puff pastry, 200g mixed mushrooms (chopped), 100g spinach, 1 onion (finely chopped), 2 garlic cloves (minced), 1 egg (beaten for glazing), salt and pepper (to taste)

Instructions:

1. Preheat the oven to 200°C (fan).
2. In a pan, sauté the onion and garlic until soft. Add the mushrooms and spinach, cooking until the moisture has evaporated.
3. Roll out the puff pastry and place the mushroom mixture in the centre.
4. Fold the pastry over the filling and seal the edges. Brush with beaten egg.
5. Bake for 35 minutes until golden brown. Serve with gravy or salad for a hearty meal!

Nutritional Info: Calories: 450 | Fat: 30g | Carbs: 30g | Protein: 10g

HOMEMADE GNOCCHI

Prep: 15 mins | Cook: 5 mins | Serves: 2

Cooking Function: Boil

Ingredients:

UK: 250g potatoes (peeled and cubed), 80g plain flour, 1 egg (beaten), salt (to taste)

Instructions:

1. Boil the potatoes in salted water until tender, then drain and mash.

2. In a bowl, mix the mashed potatoes with flour, beaten egg, and salt until a dough forms.

3. Roll the dough into long strips and cut into small pieces.

4. Boil in salted water until the gnocchi float to the surface, then drain. Serve with your favourite sauce!

Nutritional Info: Calories: 300 | Fat: 1g | Carbs: 60g | Protein: 8g

BEEF STROGANOFF

Prep: 10 mins | Cook: 20 mins | Serves: 2

Cooking Function: Sauté

Ingredients:

UK: 200g beef steak (sliced), 150g mushrooms (sliced), 1 onion (finely chopped), 100ml beef stock, 100ml sour cream, 2 tablespoons olive oil, salt and pepper (to taste), 1 tablespoon Dijon mustard

Instructions:

1. Heat olive oil in a pan and sauté the onions and mushrooms until soft.

2. Add the beef slices and cook until browned.

3. Pour in the beef stock and stir in the Dijon mustard, letting it simmer for 5 minutes.

4. Remove from heat and stir in the sour cream, seasoning to taste. Serve over rice or pasta for a comforting meal!

Nutritional Info: Calories: 550 | Fat: 30g | Carbs: 25g | Protein: 40g

CHAPTER 9: CAKES AND COOKIES

EASY CHOCOLATE CAKE

Prep: 10 mins | Cook: 30 mins | Serves: 8

Cooking Function: Bake

Ingredients:

UK: 200g self-raising flour, 200g caster sugar, 200g unsalted butter (softened), 4 large eggs, 50g cocoa powder, 1 teaspoon vanilla extract, 100ml milk, pinch of salt

Instructions:

1. Preheat the oven to 180°C (fan). Grease and line a round cake tin.
2. In a large mixing bowl, cream together the softened butter and caster sugar until light and fluffy.
3. Beat in the eggs, one at a time, adding a spoonful of flour with each egg to prevent curdling.
4. Sift in the self-raising flour, cocoa powder, and salt, then fold in gently.
5. Stir in the milk and vanilla extract until smooth.
6. Pour the batter into the prepared cake tin and bake for 25-30 minutes, or until a skewer inserted comes out clean.
7. Let it cool in the tin for 10 minutes before transferring to a wire rack to cool completely.
8. Serve it plain or with a dusting of icing sugar for a delicious treat!

Nutritional Info: Calories: 350 | Fat: 20g | Carbs: 45g | Protein: 6g

VICTORIA SPONGE

Prep: 10 mins | Cook: 25 mins | Serves: 8

Cooking Function: Bake

Ingredients:

UK: 200g unsalted butter (softened), 200g caster sugar, 4 large eggs, 200g self-raising flour, 1 teaspoon baking powder, 2 tablespoons milk, 100g strawberry jam, icing sugar (for dusting)

Instructions:

1. Preheat the oven to 180°C (fan). Grease and line two round cake tins.
2. In a mixing bowl, beat together the softened butter and sugar until creamy.
3. Add the eggs, one by one, mixing well after each addition.
4. Sift in the self-raising flour and baking powder, then fold in gently.
5. Stir in the milk until the batter is smooth.
6. Divide the mixture evenly between the two cake tins and bake for 20-25 minutes.
7. Once baked, let the cakes cool in the tins for 10 minutes, then transfer to a wire rack.
8. Spread strawberry jam on one cake, top with the other, and dust with icing sugar before serving!

Nutritional Info: Calories: 300 | Fat: 15g | Carbs: 38g | Protein: 5g

CHOCOLATE CHIP COOKIES

Prep: 10 mins | Cook: 12 mins | Serves: 12

Cooking Function: Bake

Ingredients:

UK: 125g unsalted butter (softened), 100g brown sugar, 50g caster sugar, 1 large egg, 1 teaspoon vanilla extract, 200g plain flour, 1 teaspoon baking soda, 100g chocolate chips, pinch of salt

Instructions:

1. Preheat the oven to 180°C (fan). Line a baking tray with parchment paper.
2. In a bowl, cream the softened butter, brown sugar, and caster sugar together until fluffy.
3. Beat in the egg and vanilla extract until well combined.
4. Sift in the plain flour, baking soda, and salt, then mix until just combined.
5. Fold in the chocolate chips.
6. Scoop tablespoon-sized amounts of dough onto the prepared tray, spacing them apart.
7. Bake for 10-12 minutes until golden brown. Let them cool on the tray for a few minutes before transferring to a wire rack.
8. Enjoy these gooey delights with a cup of tea or coffee!

Nutritional Info: Calories: 150 | Fat: 7g | Carbs: 20g | Protein: 2g

BANANA BREAD

Prep: 15 mins | Cook: 60 mins | Serves: 8

Cooking Function: Bake

Ingredients:

UK: 3 ripe bananas (mashed), 200g plain flour, 75g unsalted butter (melted), 100g brown sugar, 1 large egg, 1 teaspoon baking soda, 1 teaspoon vanilla extract, pinch of salt

Instructions:

1. Preheat the oven to 175°C (fan). Grease a loaf tin.
2. In a bowl, mix the melted butter and sugar until combined.
3. Stir in the mashed bananas and beaten egg.
4. Sift in the plain flour, baking soda, and salt, then fold gently until just mixed.
5. Pour the mixture into the prepared loaf tin.
6. Bake for 50-60 minutes, or until a skewer comes out clean.
7. Let it cool in the tin for 10 minutes, then transfer to a wire rack.
8. Slice and serve as a sweet snack or breakfast option!

Nutritional Info: Calories: 200 | Fat: 8g | Carbs: 30g | Protein: 3g

FLAPJACKS

Prep: 10 mins | Cook: 25 mins | Serves: 8

Cooking Function: Bake

Ingredients:

UK: 200g rolled oats, 100g unsalted butter, 75g brown sugar, 3 tablespoons golden syrup, 50g dried fruits (optional), pinch of salt

Instructions:

1. Preheat the oven to 180°C (fan). Grease a baking tray.
2. In a saucepan, melt the butter, sugar, and golden syrup over low heat.
3. Once melted, remove from heat and stir in the rolled oats and salt (and dried fruits, if using).
4. Mix well until combined.
5. Spread the mixture into the prepared baking tray, pressing down firmly.
6. Bake for 20-25 minutes until golden brown.
7. Allow to cool for 10 minutes before cutting into squares.
8. These make a perfect on-the-go snack!

Nutritional Info: Calories: 250 | Fat: 12g | Carbs: 34g | Protein: 4g

BROWNIES

Prep: 15 mins | Cook: 30 mins | Serves: 12

Cooking Function: Bake

Ingredients:

UK: 200g dark chocolate (chopped), 150g unsalted butter, 250g caster sugar, 4 large eggs, 100g plain flour, 1 teaspoon vanilla extract, pinch of salt

Instructions:

1. Preheat the oven to 180°C (fan). Grease and line a square baking tin.
2. Melt the dark chocolate and butter together in a bowl over a pan of simmering water.
3. In a separate bowl, whisk the sugar and eggs until fluffy.
4. Pour the melted chocolate mixture into the egg mixture and stir until combined.
5. Sift in the plain flour and salt, folding gently until just mixed.
6. Pour the batter into the prepared tin and bake for 25-30 minutes.
7. Allow to cool before slicing into squares. Serve with ice cream for a decadent dessert!

Nutritional Info: Calories: 300 | Fat: 18g | Carbs: 35g | Protein: 5g

MUFFINS

Prep: 10 mins | Cook: 20 mins | Serves: 12

Cooking Function: Bake

Ingredients:

UK: 250g self-raising flour, 100g caster sugar, 1 teaspoon baking powder, 2 large eggs, 125ml milk, 75ml vegetable oil, 100g chocolate chips or berries (optional)

Instructions:

1. Preheat the oven to 180°C (fan). Line a muffin tray with cases.
2. In a mixing bowl, combine the flour, sugar, and baking powder.
3. In another bowl, whisk together the eggs, milk, and oil.
4. Pour the wet ingredients into the dry ingredients and mix until just combined.
5. Fold in chocolate chips or berries if using.
6. Spoon the mixture into the muffin cases, filling them about 2/3 full.
7. Bake for 15-20 minutes until golden brown.
8. Let them cool slightly before enjoying these tasty treats!

Nutritional Info: Calories: 180 | Fat: 7g | Carbs: 25g | Protein: 3g

SHORTBREAD

Prep: 10 mins | Cook: 20 mins | Serves: 16

Cooking Function: Bake

Ingredients:

UK: 200g unsalted butter (softened), 100g caster sugar, 300g plain flour, pinch of salt

Instructions:

1. Preheat the oven to 150°C (fan). Line a baking tray with parchment paper.
2. In a bowl, cream the softened butter and sugar until smooth.
3. Gradually add the plain flour and salt, mixing until a dough forms.
4. Roll out the dough to about 1cm thick and cut into shapes.
5. Place the shapes onto the prepared tray.
6. Bake for 20 minutes or until lightly golden.
7. Allow to cool before enjoying with a cuppa!

Nutritional Info: Calories: 150 | Fat: 10g | Carbs: 14g | Protein: 2g

ROCKY ROAD

Prep: 15 mins | Cook: 10 mins | Serves: 12

Cooking Function: Chill

Ingredients:

UK: 200g dark chocolate, 100g unsalted butter, 100g digestive biscuits (broken), 100g marshmallows, 50g dried fruits (optional), icing sugar (for dusting)

Instructions:

1. Melt the dark chocolate and butter together in a bowl over a pan of simmering water.
2. Once melted, remove from heat and stir in the broken biscuits, marshmallows, and dried fruits (if using).
3. Press the mixture into a lined square baking tin.
4. Refrigerate for at least 2 hours until set.
5. Dust with icing sugar before cutting into squares.
6. Enjoy this no-bake treat at parties or movie nights!

Nutritional Info: Calories: 250 | Fat: 12g | Carbs: 35g | Protein: 3g

LEMON DRIZZLE CAKE

Prep: 10 mins | Cook: 40 mins | Serves: 8

Cooking Function: Bake

Ingredients:

UK: 200g unsalted butter (softened), 200g caster sugar, 4 large eggs, 200g self-raising flour, zest of 1 lemon, 50ml lemon juice, 100g icing sugar (for drizzle)

Instructions:

1. Preheat the oven to 180°C (fan). Grease a loaf tin.
2. In a mixing bowl, cream together the softened butter and caster sugar until fluffy.
3. Add the eggs, one at a time, mixing well after each addition.
4. Fold in the self-raising flour, lemon zest, and lemon juice until well combined.
5. Pour the mixture into the prepared tin and bake for 35-40 minutes.
6. While the cake is cooling, mix the icing sugar with lemon juice to make a drizzle.
7. Once cooled, drizzle the icing over the cake.
8. Slice and enjoy this refreshing treat!

Nutritional Info: Calories: 300 | Fat: 15g | Carbs: 40g | Protein: 5g

CARROT CAKE

Prep: 15 mins | Cook: 40 mins | Serves: 10

Cooking Function: Bake

Ingredients:

UK: 250g grated carrots, 200g self-raising flour, 200g caster sugar, 3 large eggs, 150ml vegetable oil, 1 teaspoon cinnamon, 50g walnuts (chopped, optional), icing sugar (for dusting)

Instructions:

1. Preheat the oven to 180°C (fan). Grease a round cake tin.
2. In a large bowl, mix the grated carrots, flour, sugar, eggs, oil, and cinnamon until well combined.
3. Fold in the walnuts, if using.
4. Pour the mixture into the prepared tin and bake for 30-40 minutes.
5. Allow to cool for 10 minutes before transferring to a wire rack.
6. Dust with icing sugar before serving.
7. This moist cake is perfect with a cup of tea!

Nutritional Info: Calories: 320 | Fat: 18g | Carbs: 40g | Protein: 6g

NO-BAKE TRAY BAKE

Prep: 10 mins | Cook: 0 mins | Serves: 12

Cooking Function: Chill

Ingredients:

UK: 250g digestive biscuits (crushed), 100g unsalted butter (melted), 150g milk chocolate (melted), 100g marshmallows, 50g dried fruits (optional), icing sugar (for dusting)

Instructions:

1. In a bowl, mix the crushed biscuits and melted butter until combined.
2. Press the mixture into a lined baking tray.
3. In another bowl, mix the melted chocolate with marshmallows and dried fruits (if using).
4. Pour the chocolate mixture over the biscuit base, spreading it evenly.
5. Refrigerate for at least 2 hours until set.
6. Dust with icing sugar before cutting into squares.
7. This is an easy and delicious treat for any occasion!

Nutritional Info: Calories: 250 | Fat: 12g | Carbs: 35g | Protein: 3g

ENERGY BALLS

Prep: 15 mins | Cook: 0 mins | Serves: 12

Cooking Function: Chill

Ingredients:

UK: 200g rolled oats, 100g peanut butter, 50g honey, 50g chocolate chips, 50g dried fruits, pinch of salt

Instructions:

1. In a mixing bowl, combine all the ingredients and mix well until combined.
2. Roll the mixture into small balls, about the size of a walnut.
3. Place the energy balls on a lined tray.
4. Refrigerate for at least 30 minutes to firm up.
5. Enjoy these nutritious bites as a quick snack or pre-workout fuel!

Nutritional Info: Calories: 120 | Fat: 5g | Carbs: 15g | Protein: 3g

CHAPTER 10: PROPER PUDS

APPLE CRUMBLE

Prep: 15 mins | Cook: 40 mins | Serves: 4

Cooking Function: Bake

Ingredients:

UK: 4 medium apples (peeled, cored, and sliced), 100g brown sugar, 200g plain flour, 100g butter (cubed), 50g rolled oats, 1 teaspoon cinnamon, a pinch of salt

Instructions:

1. Preheat the oven to 180°C (fan).
2. In a bowl, toss the sliced apples with brown sugar and cinnamon until well coated.
3. Spread the apples in an even layer in a baking dish.
4. In another bowl, rub the butter into the flour until it resembles breadcrumbs.
5. Stir in the oats, cinnamon, and salt.
6. Sprinkle the crumble mixture over the apples.
7. Bake in the oven for 30-35 minutes, or until the top is golden and the apples are bubbling.
8. Serve warm with custard or ice cream for a comforting dessert!

Nutritional Info: Calories: 280 | Fat: 12g | Carbs: 40g | Protein: 3g

BREAD AND BUTTER PUDDING

Prep: 10 mins | Cook: 40 mins | Serves: 4

Cooking Function: Bake

Ingredients:

UK: 8 slices of bread (preferably stale), 100g butter, 4 large eggs, 500ml milk, 100g sugar, 1 teaspoon vanilla extract, a pinch of nutmeg, sultanas (optional)

Instructions:

1. Preheat the oven to 160°C (fan).
2. Butter the bread slices generously on one side.
3. Cut the bread into triangles and layer them in a greased baking dish, sprinkling sultanas between layers if using.
4. In a bowl, whisk together the eggs, milk, sugar, vanilla extract, and nutmeg until combined.
5. Pour the mixture over the layered bread and allow it to soak for about 15 minutes.
6. Bake for 30-35 minutes until the pudding is golden and set.
7. Serve warm with cream or custard for a classic treat!

Nutritional Info: Calories: 320 | Fat: 15g | Carbs: 40g | Protein: 8g

MICROWAVE MUG CAKE

Prep: 5 mins | Cook: 1 min | Serves: 1

Cooking Function: Microwave

Ingredients:

UK: 4 tablespoons plain flour, 4 tablespoons sugar, 2 tablespoons cocoa powder, 1 egg, 3 tablespoons milk, 3 tablespoons vegetable oil, a splash of vanilla extract, chocolate chips (optional)

Instructions:

1. In a large microwave-safe mug, whisk together the flour, sugar, cocoa powder, and egg until smooth.
2. Add the milk, vegetable oil, and vanilla extract, mixing well.
3. Stir in chocolate chips if you like a gooey centre.
4. Microwave on high for 1 minute, checking for doneness. If it's still wet, microwave for an additional 10 seconds at a time.
5. Let it cool for a minute before devouring this quick dessert!

Nutritional Info: Calories: 400 | Fat: 18g | Carbs: 54g | Protein: 8g

QUICK FRUIT COBBLER

Prep: 10 mins | Cook: 30 mins | Serves: 4

Cooking Function: Bake

Ingredients:

UK: 400g mixed berries (frozen or fresh), 100g sugar, 200g self-raising flour, 100g butter (cubed), 150ml milk, 1 teaspoon vanilla extract

Instructions:

1. Preheat the oven to 180°C (fan).
2. In a baking dish, mix the berries with half of the sugar and set aside.
3. In a bowl, rub the butter into the flour until crumbly.
4. Stir in the remaining sugar, milk, and vanilla extract until just combined.
5. Pour the batter over the berries, spreading it evenly.
6. Bake for 25-30 minutes until the top is golden and the berries are bubbling.
7. Serve warm with ice cream for a delightful dessert!

Nutritional Info: Calories: 320 | Fat: 12g | Carbs: 50g | Protein: 5g

NO-BAKE CHEESECAKE

Prep: 15 mins | Cook: 0 mins | Serves: 8

Cooking Function: Chill

Ingredients:

UK: 250g digestive biscuits (crushed), 100g butter (melted), 300g cream cheese, 100g icing sugar, 1 teaspoon vanilla extract, 200ml double cream, fruit topping (optional)

Instructions:

1. In a bowl, mix the crushed biscuits with melted butter until combined.
2. Press the mixture into the bottom of a springform tin to form the base.
3. In another bowl, beat together the cream cheese, icing sugar, and vanilla extract until smooth.
4. Whip the double cream until it forms soft peaks, then fold it into the cream cheese mixture.
5. Pour the filling onto the biscuit base and smooth it out.
6. Chill in the fridge for at least 4 hours, or until set.
7. Top with your choice of fruit before serving for a refreshing finish!

Nutritional Info: Calories: 380 | Fat: 28g | Carbs: 30g | Protein: 5g

CHOCOLATE MOUSSE

Prep: 10 mins | Cook: 0 mins | Serves: 4

Cooking Function: Chill

Ingredients:

UK: 200g dark chocolate (broken into pieces), 3 large eggs, 50g sugar, 200ml double cream, a pinch of salt

Instructions:

1. Melt the dark chocolate in a heatproof bowl over simmering water.
2. In another bowl, whisk the eggs with sugar until frothy and pale.
3. Once the chocolate has cooled slightly, mix it into the egg mixture until combined.
4. In a separate bowl, whip the double cream to soft peaks.
5. Gently fold the whipped cream into the chocolate mixture until just combined.
6. Spoon into serving glasses and chill for at least 2 hours.
7. Enjoy this indulgent dessert on its own or with berries!

Nutritional Info: Calories: 320 | Fat: 25g | Carbs: 15g | Protein: 6g

RICE PUDDING

Prep: 5 mins | Cook: 1 hour | Serves: 4

Cooking Function: Simmer

Ingredients:

UK: 200g short-grain rice, 1 litre whole milk, 100g sugar, 1 teaspoon vanilla extract, a pinch of salt, cinnamon (for serving)

Instructions:

1. In a saucepan, combine the rice, milk, sugar, vanilla extract, and salt.
2. Bring to a gentle simmer over low heat, stirring frequently.
3. Cook for about 45-60 minutes, until the rice is tender and the mixture thickens.
4. Remove from heat and let it cool slightly.
5. Serve warm or cold, dusted with cinnamon for a comforting dessert!

Nutritional Info: Calories: 250 | Fat: 7g | Carbs: 42g | Protein: 8g

ETON MESS

Prep: 10 mins | Cook: 0 mins | Serves: 4

Cooking Function: Chill

Ingredients:

UK: 300g strawberries (hulled and halved), 200ml double cream, 2 meringue nests (crumbled), 50g sugar

Instructions:

1. In a bowl, whip the double cream with sugar until soft peaks form.
2. In another bowl, gently mix the strawberries with the crumbled meringue.
3. Fold the strawberry and meringue mixture into the whipped cream.
4. Spoon the Eton Mess into serving glasses.
5. Chill for a short while before serving for a refreshing dessert!

Nutritional Info: Calories: 290 | Fat: 16g | Carbs: 35g | Protein: 3g

STICKY TOFFEE PUDDING

Prep: 20 mins | Cook: 30 mins | Serves: 6

Cooking Function: Bake

Ingredients:

UK: 200g dried dates (pitted and chopped), 250ml boiling water, 100g dark brown sugar, 100g butter (softened), 2 large eggs, 200g self-raising flour, 1 teaspoon baking powder, a pinch of salt, 200ml double cream (for sauce)

Instructions:

1. Preheat the oven to 180°C (fan).
2. Soak the chopped dates in boiling water for 10 minutes, then mash to a puree.
3. In a bowl, cream together the butter and brown sugar until light and fluffy.
4. Beat in the eggs one at a time, then mix in the date puree.
5. Fold in the flour, baking powder, and salt until just combined.
6. Pour the mixture into a greased baking dish and bake for 25-30 minutes until golden.
7. Meanwhile, heat the double cream in a saucepan until just simmering, pour it over the pudding to serve.

Nutritional Info: Calories: 450 | Fat: 22g | Carbs: 60g | Protein: 6g

PANCAKES

Prep: 10 mins | Cook: 15 mins | Serves: 4

Cooking Function: Fry

Ingredients:

UK: 200g plain flour, 2 large eggs, 300ml milk, 1 tablespoon sugar, 1 teaspoon baking powder, a pinch of salt, butter (for frying)

Instructions:

1. In a bowl, whisk together the flour, sugar, baking powder, and salt.
2. Make a well in the centre and add the eggs and milk, whisking until smooth.
3. Heat a non-stick frying pan over medium heat and melt a little butter.
4. Pour in a ladleful of batter and cook for 2-3 minutes until bubbles form on the surface.
5. Flip and cook for another 1-2 minutes until golden.
6. Repeat with the remaining batter, keeping the pancakes warm.
7. Serve with your choice of syrup, fruit, or chocolate spread!

Nutritional Info: Calories: 210 | Fat: 8g | Carbs: 30g | Protein: 6g

ICE CREAM SUNDAE

Prep: 5 mins | Cook: 0 mins | Serves: 2

Cooking Function: Chill

Ingredients:

UK: 4 scoops of ice cream (flavour of your choice), 100ml chocolate sauce, 50g chopped nuts, whipped cream (optional), cherries (for topping)

Instructions:

1. In a sundae glass, place two scoops of ice cream at the bottom.
2. Drizzle with chocolate sauce and sprinkle with chopped nuts.
3. Add the remaining scoops of ice cream on top.
4. Finish with a dollop of whipped cream and a cherry on top.
5. Enjoy your decadent sundae right away!

Nutritional Info: Calories: 450 | Fat: 25g | Carbs: 50g | Protein: 6g

FRUIT CRUMBLE

Prep: 15 mins | Cook: 30 mins | Serves: 4

Cooking Function: Bake

Ingredients:

UK: 500g mixed fruit (e.g., apples, berries, or rhubarb), 100g sugar, 150g plain flour, 100g butter (cubed), 50g oats, 1 teaspoon cinnamon

Instructions:

1. Preheat the oven to 180°C (fan).
2. Toss the mixed fruit with half of the sugar and place in a baking dish.
3. In a bowl, rub the butter into the flour until it resembles breadcrumbs.
4. Stir in the oats, cinnamon, and remaining sugar.
5. Spread the crumble mixture over the fruit evenly.
6. Bake for 25-30 minutes until golden and bubbly.
7. Serve warm with custard or cream!

Nutritional Info: Calories: 310 | Fat: 12g | Carbs: 45g | Protein: 5g

QUICK TIRAMISU

Prep: 15 mins | Cook: 0 mins | Serves: 4

Cooking Function: Chill

Ingredients:

UK: 250g mascarpone cheese, 200ml double cream, 50g sugar, 1 teaspoon vanilla extract, 1 cup strong coffee (cooled), 200g ladyfinger biscuits, cocoa powder (for dusting)

Instructions:

1. In a bowl, whisk together the mascarpone, double cream, sugar, and vanilla extract until smooth.
2. Dip each ladyfinger in the cooled coffee briefly, then layer them in a serving dish.
3. Spread half of the mascarpone mixture over the ladyfingers.
4. Repeat the layers with the remaining ladyfingers and mascarpone.
5. Chill for at least 2 hours before serving, dusting with cocoa powder.
6. Enjoy this delightful dessert with friends!

Nutritional Info: Calories: 400 | Fat: 30g | Carbs: 30g | Protein: 6g

SUBSTITUTION CHARTS

Common Ingredient Swaps

Need This	Use This Instead
Butter	Margarine, oil, apple sauce (in baking)
Fresh herbs	Dried herbs (use 1/3 amount)
Double cream	Single cream + butter, Greek yoghurt
Eggs (in baking)	Mashed banana, apple sauce
Fresh milk	UHT milk, oat milk
White wine (cooking)	Stock + lemon juice
Fresh garlic	Garlic powder, lazy garlic
Buttermilk	Milk + lemon juice
Fresh vegetables	Frozen vegetables

Budget-Friendly Protein Swaps

Instead of	Try Using
Chicken breast	Chicken thighs (cheaper)
Beef mince	Mixed mince, Quorn mince
Fresh fish	Tinned fish, fish fingers
Lamb	Cheaper cuts of beef
Prawns	Tinned tuna, fish pieces

KITCHEN EQUIPMENT CHECKLIST

Essential Starter Kit (Total budget £50-£70)

[ ] Chef's knife (£10-15)
[ ] 2 chopping boards (£5-8)
[ ] Large saucepan (£8-10)
[ ] Frying pan (£10-12)
[ ] Wooden spoon set (£3-5)
[ ] Measuring jug (£3)
[ ] Can opener (£2)
[ ] Tea towels x3 (£3)
[ ] Colander (£3)
[ ] Peeler (£2)

Nice to Have (When you can afford it)

[ ] Hand blender (£15-20)
[ ] Rice cooker (£20-25)
[ ] Food storage containers (£10)
[ ] Baking trays (£5-8)
[ ] Kitchen scales (£8-10)

COMMON COOKING PROBLEMS SOLVED

Problem: Pasta Issues

* **Too sticky:** Add oil to water, stir more
* **Overcooked:** Set a timer, taste test
* **Stuck together:** Use more water, and stir initially

Problem: Rice Troubles

* **Too wet:** Less water, longer cooking
* **Burnt bottom:** Lower heat, proper pan
* **Undercooked:** More water, longer time

Problem: Sauce Disasters

* **Too thin:** Simmer longer, add cornflour
* **Too thick:** Add water gradually
* **Lumpy:** Use a whisk, strain if needed

Problem: Burning Issues

* **Pan too hot:** Lower heat, use timer
* **Food sticking:** More oil, non-stick pan
* **Burning bottom:** Stir more, lower heat

KITCHEN SAFETY CHECKLIST

Daily Checks
[ ] Tea towels away from the hob
[ ] Pan handles turned in
[ ] Floor dry and clear
[ ] Knives stored safely
[ ] Windows open for ventilation

Fire Safety
[ ] Know where the fire blanket is
[ ] Learn how to use an extinguisher
[ ] Never leave cooking unattended
[ ] Keep toaster away from curtains
[ ] Test smoke alarm weekly

FOOD HYGIENE BASICS

Personal Hygiene
1. Wash hands:
  * Before cooking
  * After handling raw meat
  * After touching the bin

  * After touching the phone

2. Tie back long hair
3. Clean apron/clothes
4. No rings/watches while cooking

KITCHEN HYGIENE

1. Clean as you go:
  * Wipe spills immediately
  * Wash used equipment
  * Clear workspace regularly

2. Food Storage:
  * Check temperatures (fridge 0-5°C)
  * Store raw meat at the bottom
  * Keep cooked/raw separate

Here's a nutritionally balanced 60-day meal plan for students, arranged by week and focusing on providing a variety of nutrients throughout the day. Each week contains a balance of proteins, healthy fats, carbohydrates, and plenty of fruits and vegetables. This plan includes breakfast, lunch, appetisers, and a special Sunday dinner.

WEEK 1

DAYS	BREAKFAST	LUNCH	Appetizer	DINNER
MONDAY	Overnight Oats with Berries	Tuna Pasta Bake with Spinach	Homemade Hummus with Veggie Sticks	Grilled Chicken Burger with Sweet Potato Fries
TUESDAY	Banana and Almond Butter on Wholegrain Toast	Lentil and Vegetable Soup	Crispy Baked Chickpeas	Chilli Con Carne with Brown Rice
WEDNESDAY	Greek Yogurt with Honey and Nuts	Egg Fried Rice with Mixed Vegetables	Vegetable Spring Rolls	One-pot chicken and Rice
THURSDAY	Scrambled Eggs with Spinach and Tomatoes	Quinoa Salad with Chickpeas and Feta	Roasted Vegetable Platter	Veggie Stir-Fry with Tofu and Brown Rice
FRIDAY	Smoothie Bowl with Mixed Fruits	Wholegrain Pasta Arrabiata with Zucchini	Crispy Prawns with Dipping Sauce	Baked Cod with Mediterranean Vegetables
SATURDAY	Full English Breakfast (with Grilled Tomatoes)	Budget Bean Chilli with Rice	Nachos with Guacamole and Salsa	Mediterranean Chicken with Quinoa
SUNDAY (SPECIAL DINNER)	No-Bake Breakfast Energy Bars	Chickpea Salad with Avocado	Spinach and Artichoke Dip with Wholegrain Crisps	Toad in the Hole with Gravy

WEEK 2

DAYS	BREAKFAST	LUNCH	Appetizer	DINNER
MONDAY	Overnight Chia Pudding with Fresh Fruit	Chicken Curry with Cauliflower Rice	Stuffed Bell Peppers	Vegetable and Bean Stew
TUESDAY	Oatmeal with Berries and Nuts	Jacket Potato with Tuna and Salad	Homemade Kebab Wrap with Tzatziki	Roast Chicken with Sweet Potatoes
WEDNESDAY	Fruit Smoothie with Spinach and Banana	Quinoa and Black Bean Salad	Cheese and Wholegrain Crackers	One-pot mac and Cheese with Broccoli
THURSDAY	Avocado Toast on Wholegrain Bread	Tomato and Lentil Soup	Crispy Onion Bhajis	Sweet Potato and Chickpea Curry
FRIDAY	Pancakes with Maple Syrup and Berries	Sausage and Bean Casserole	Mini Quiches with Veggies	Beef Stew and Dumplings
SATURDAY	Granola with Yogurt and Fruit	Chickpea and Spinach Patties	Crispy Cauliflower Bites	Chicken and Leek Pie
SUNDAY (SPECIAL DINNER)	Lemon Drizzle Cake (slice)	Pasta Salad with Veggies and Feta	Buffalo Cauliflower Bites	Sticky Toffee Pudding

WEEK 3

DAYS	BREAKFAST	LUNCH	Appetizer	DINNER
MONDAY	Berry Muffins with Wholegrain Flour	Prawn and Mango Salad	Roasted Chickpeas	Mushroom Risotto with Peas
TUESDAY	Smoothie Bowl with Spinach and Avocado	Veggie Quesadillas with Salsa	Crispy Kale Chips	Stir-fried beef with Broccoli
WEDNESDAY	Scrambled Tofu with Spinach and Tomatoes	Lentil Salad with Roasted Veggies	Vegetable Samosas	Baked Vegetable Lasagne
THURSDAY	Peanut Butter and Banana Overnight Oats	Chicken Caesar Salad with Wholegrain Croutons	Crispy Sweet Potato Fries	Stuffed Peppers with Quinoa and Black Beans
FRIDAY	Yogurt Parfait with Granola	Chickpea Curry with Brown Rice	Crispy Eggplant Chips	Fish Tacos with Slaw
SATURDAY	Fruit and Nut Overnight Oats	Mushroom Stroganoff	Vegetable Spring Rolls	Air-Fried Vegetable Kebabs
SUNDAY (SPECIAL DINNER)	Apple Crumble (for a treat)	Mediterranean Stuffed Courgettes	Sharing a Platter of Dips and Veggies	No-Bake Cheesecake

WEEK 4

DAYS	BREAKFAST	LUNCH	Appetizer	DINNER
MONDAY	Nut Butter on Wholegrain Toast	Quinoa Salad with Feta and Cherry Tomatoes	Crispy Zucchini Fritters	Sweet Potato and Black Bean Enchiladas
TUESDAY	Overnight Oats with Apple and Cinnamon	Lentil and Vegetable Soup	Mini Corn Dogs	Grilled Chicken Fajitas with Peppers
WEDNESDAY	Spinach and Feta Wrap	Quinoa Salad with Roasted Veggies	Crispy Broccoli Bites	Vegetable Stir-Fry with Tofu
THURSDAY	Smoothie Bowl with Bananas and Spinach	Tomato Pasta with Grilled Veggies	Garlic Bread with Hummus	Baked Chicken Thighs with Vegetables
FRIDAY	Yogurt with Granola and Berries	Veggie Burger with Sweet Potato Fries	Crispy Potato Skins	Grilled Fish with Asparagus
SATURDAY	Fruit and Yogurt Parfait	Chickpea Salad with Avocado	Stuffed Jalapeño Poppers	Vegetable Pizza with a Wholegrain Base
SUNDAY (SPECIAL DINNER)	Pancakes with Fresh Fruit	Chickpea and Spinach Stew	Nachos with Salsa	Eton Mess

WEEK 5

DAYS	BREAKFAST	LUNCH	Appetizer	DINNER
MONDAY	Baked Oatmeal with Berries	Tuna Salad Wraps with Leafy Greens	Veggie Chips	Chicken Katsu with Steamed Rice
TUESDAY	Oatmeal with Peanut Butter and Bananas	Roasted Vegetable Quinoa Bowl	Cheese Quesadillas with Salsa	Sweet Potato and Chickpea Curry
WEDNESDAY	Smoothie with Spinach, Banana, and Almond Milk	Egg Salad Sandwich with Lettuce	Veggie Spring Rolls with Dipping Sauce	Stir-fried beef with Bell Peppers
THURSDAY	Yogurt with Fruit and Nuts	Grilled Chicken Salad with Avocado	Mini Quiches with Spinach	Vegetable and Bean Stew
FRIDAY	Fruit and Nut Overnight Oats	Wholegrain Wrap with Hummus and Veggies	Crispy Cauliflower Bites	Chicken Stir-Fry with Broccoli and Carrots
SATURDAY	Breakfast Burrito with Eggs and Veggies	Quinoa Salad with Chickpeas	Garlic Bread with Marinara	Grilled Chicken with Mixed Vegetables
SUNDAY (SPECIAL DINNER)	Chocolate Chip Muffins (for a treat)	Chickpea Curry with Rice	Crispy Veggie Samosas	Chocolate Mousse

WEEK 6

DAYS	BREAKFAST	LUNCH	Appetizer	DINNER
MONDAY	Overnight Chia Pudding with Berries	Lentil Soup with Wholegrain Bread	Roasted Vegetable Platter	Chicken and Rice Casserole
TUESDAY	Smoothie Bowl with Mixed Fruits	Quinoa Salad with Feta	Cheese and Wholegrain Crackers	Grilled Salmon with Vegetables
WEDNESDAY	Scrambled Eggs with Spinach	Prawn and Mango Salad	Crispy Kale Chips	Veggie Stir-Fry with Tofu
THURSDAY	Peanut Butter Toast with Banana	Chickpea Salad with Avocado	Stuffed Bell Peppers	Chicken Tikka Masala with Rice
FRIDAY	Yogurt with Granola and Fresh Fruit	Tuna Pasta with Veggies	Baked Mozzarella Sticks	Beef Stir-Fry with Mixed Vegetables
SATURDAY	Pancakes with Berries	Veggie Burger with Sweet Potato Fries	Homemade Hummus with Pita	Baked Cod with Broccoli
SUNDAY (SPECIAL DINNER)	Fruit Salad with Yogurt	Quinoa Bowl with Grilled Chicken	Nachos with Salsa	Apple Crumble

WEEK 7

DAYS	BREAKFAST	LUNCH	Appetizer	DINNER
MONDAY	Overnight Oats with Almonds and Dried Fruit	Spinach and Feta Wraps	Roasted Red Pepper Hummus with Veggies	Turkey Meatballs with Wholegrain Spaghetti
TUESDAY	Smoothie with Spinach, Banana, and Oats	Chickpea and Avocado Salad	Crispy Zucchini Fries	Stuffed Peppers with Rice and Beans
WEDNESDAY	Greek Yogurt with Honey and Mixed Nuts	Vegetable Fried Rice with Tofu	Mini Spring Rolls with Sweet Chili Sauce	Baked Lemon Herb Chicken with Asparagus
THURSDAY	Scrambled Eggs with Tomato and Avocado	Quinoa Salad with Roasted Chickpeas	Spinach and Artichoke Dip with Wholegrain Crisps	Vegetable Stir-Fry with Brown Rice
FRIDAY	Pancakes with Maple Syrup and Bananas	Tuna Salad with Wholegrain Crackers	Baked Sweet Potato Wedges	Grilled Steak with Mixed Vegetables
SATURDAY	Fruit and Nut Muesli with Yogurt	Tomato and Basil Pasta	Caprese Skewers with Balsamic Drizzle	Roasted Chicken with Sweet Potato Mash
SUNDAY (SPECIAL DINNER)	Chocolate Banana Smoothie	Quinoa Bowl with Black Beans and Avocado	Pita Bread with Tzatziki	Brownies with Ice Cream

WEEK 8

DAYS	BREAKFAST	LUNCH	Appetizer	DINNER
MONDAY	Overnight Chia Pudding with Coconut and Mango	Lentil Salad with Roasted Vegetables	Cucumber and Cream Cheese Sandwiches	Chicken Fajitas with Peppers and Onions
TUESDAY	Smoothie with Mixed Berries and Yogurt	Wholegrain Pita with Falafel and Salad	Veggie Sticks with Hummus	Baked Cod with Roasted Vegetables
WEDNESDAY	Oatmeal with Peanut Butter and Banana	Quinoa Salad with Chickpeas and Spinach	Stuffed Mushrooms	Vegetable Pad Thai
THURSDAY	Spinach and Cheese Omelette	Tomato and Lentil Soup with Wholegrain Bread	Garlic Parmesan Roasted Broccoli	Grilled Chicken with Couscous and Veggies
FRIDAY	Yogurt Parfait with Granola and Berries	Chicken Caesar Wrap	Crispy Eggplant Fries	Beef and Vegetable Stir-Fry
SATURDAY	Smoothie Bowl with Tropical Fruits	Egg Salad Sandwich	Vegetable Spring Rolls	Roast Beef with Yorkshire Pudding
SUNDAY (SPECIAL DINNER)	Pancakes with Fresh Strawberries	Chickpea and Avocado Salad	Vegetable Antipasto Platter	Fruit Tart

WEEK 9

DAYS	BREAKFAST	LUNCH	Appetizer	DINNER
MONDAY	Overnight Oats with Apples and Cinnamon	Spinach and Feta Stuffed Chicken Breast	Caprese Salad	Turkey and Vegetable Stir-Fry
TUESDAY	Smoothie with Spinach, Banana, and Almond Milk	Quinoa Salad with Roasted Beets	Crispy Chickpeas	Grilled Salmon with Broccoli and Rice
WEDNESDAY	Greek Yogurt with Granola and Honey	Vegetable and Bean Soup	Pesto and Tomato Bruschetta	Chicken Alfredo Pasta
THURSDAY	Scrambled Eggs with Spinach and Feta	Chicken and Avocado Salad	Mini Vegetable Quiches	Vegetable Tacos with Black Beans
FRIDAY				
SATURDAY				
SUNDAY (SPECIAL DINNER)				

This meal plan aims to provide a well-rounded nutritional intake, focusing on variety while being budget-friendly and convenient for students. The inclusion of healthy fats, lean proteins, and plenty of vegetables ensures a balanced diet, while special Sunday dinners can add a bit of fun and enjoyment to the week. Adjustments can be made based on personal preferences, dietary restrictions, or seasonal availability of ingredients!

PRO TIPS:
* Take photos of your receipts
* Keep a running shopping list
* Plan around your schedule
* Always have backup meals
* Share costs with housemates

Remember: These are guidelines, not rules. Adapt them to fit your lifestyle and budget. The key is finding a system that works for you and sticking to it! HAPPY COOKING!

Printed in Great Britain
by Amazon

53487761R00064